D1112622

.

The Responsive Parent

The Responsive Parent

Meeting the Realities
Of Parenthood Today

Mary B. Hoover

Parents' Magazine Press
New York

International Standard Book Number 0–8193–0614–2
Library of Congress Catalog Card Number 72–2313
**Produced for Parents' Magazine Press
by Stravon Educational Press**
The Responsive Parent is being published in a
special edition as *What Makes a Good Parent?*
Manufactured in the United States of America

Contents

Preface ix

1 The Expert in Each of Us 13
The Value of Empathy · Flexibility Enters In · Picking
Up Cues · Attitudes Can Change · Using All We Know ·
Blind Spots · Individual Differences · The Meaning of
Projection · Testing Our Expertise · Aids to Growth in
Self-understanding · Professional Resources · Knowing
Our Limits

2 The World We Live In 32
Sources of Discontent · The Need to Become Involved ·
Doing Our Homework · Learning from the Young · Hid-
den Dividends · Other Challenges of the Times · It's Not
All Up to Parents

3 Preparing for a New Baby 54
Feelings Can Change · Talking Out Feelings · Serious
Doubts · Choosing an Obstetrician and Hospital · How
Will You Feed Your Baby? · Where Will the Baby
Sleep? · Choosing a Doctor for Your Baby · Planning
for a Mother's Return from the Hospital · Husband and
Wife as a Team · A Word About Equipment · Doing
Your Homework · "Rooming-in" · "Natural Child-
birth" · "Mother Love" · Some Goals to Keep in Mind

4 No Parent Is Perfect 78
Unavoidable Hardships · Life Is Like That · Our Role ·

Children's Vulnerability in Perspective • Toward a New Definition of Mental Health • Using Our Leeway Prudently • "Second Chances" • Learning from Mistakes • Asking What We Should of Ourselves • Making and Living with the "Hard" Decisions

5 What Makes Johnny "Behave"? **97**
Keeping Children Safe • Nurturing Self-esteem • Inculcating Respect for the Rights of Others • Encouraging Growth Toward Independence • The Development of Good "Inner Controls" • Building Healthy Attitudes Toward Authority • "Permissiveness" • Punishment • Standing Our Ground • Mothers and Discipline • Accepting the Need for Continuing Confrontation

6 Parental Example: How It Rubs Off **119**
What Is a Role Model? • What Rubs Off • The Effectiveness of Models • When Actions Speak Louder Than Words • Explaining Our Behavior • Age Makes a Difference • Sexual Identity • Hidden Assets • The Whole Picture Counts

7 Is Anybody Listening? **135**
Words Are Important • Children Must Feel Respected • It Takes Two to Tango • Being Good Listeners • Why They Don't "Listen" • Getting Our Message Straight • Mixed Messages • Getting Their Messages Straight • Getting Through to Each Other

8 Tapping a Child's Potential **150**
A Good Self-image Is Essential • Knowing How Children Develop • The Badge of Competence • Keeping Expectations Flexible • Knowing Our Child's Own Way of Doing Things • Knowing What Our Child Is Coping With • About Pushing • Evaluating Real Challenges • Real Weaknesses • Talents • Nothing Succeeds Like Success

9 The Beautiful Times **172**
Much Eludes Explanation • Is It Inborn? • The "Happy" Child • Spontaneous Delight • Celebrations • Joy and

Sorrow • Implications for Parents • Facing Up to Our
Own Feelings • Fun and Responsibility

10 **Having the Children You Want—**
and No More 188
Family Planning as a Social Responsibility • Medical
Considerations • Other Considerations • Aren't Large
Families Good for the Children? • The "Pill" • But How
Safe Is It? • The IUD • The Diaphragm with Spermicidal
Jelly or Cream • The Condom • Vaginal Foams, Creams,
Jellies, and Foaming Tablets • What the Future May
Hold • Rhythm Method • Sterilization • Abortion •
Treatment for Infertility • Adoption

11 **Our Needs in Perspective** 215
The Trap of Thinking in Terms of Opposites • How Our
Way of Viewing Problems Matters • It Is Not Always
So Easy • Avoiding Unnecessary Resentment • Over-
protection • The Temptation to Live Through Our
Children • Fulfillment in Work • Fulfillment in Mar-
riage • Divorce • One-parent Families • Disappointments
and Lasting Difficulties • Accepting Our Children and
Ourselves

Bibliography and Suggested Reading 241

Index 249

Preface

NOT LONG AGO a fourteen-year-old boy clumped into the living room of his home upon awakening and demanded, rubbing his eyes sleepily, "How's the avocado doing?" The plant seemed to have shot up several inches overnight, as such plants often do in the early months after the shoot pokes through. The boy's sleepy look changed to one of wonderment, mixed seconds later with concern. He ran a forefinger over the earth in the pot and headed for the kitchen. Returning with the watering can, he said, "They need a lot of water."

His mother, watching this procedure, was struck by the coincidence of the push to grow and the push to nurture growth: a seed sprouting breathtakingly; a boy sprouting equally so; and that boy touchingly bent on caring for the seed's issue. Was it a temporary matter of the boy's tending to identify with any similarly fast-developing organism? Or was it more than that: an expression of an urge we all have, male no less than female, to be nurturing where growing things are concerned?

Nobody knows, of course. In watching and helping our children grow, we often feel that we are being exposed, in microcosm, to the most profound and tantalizing mysteries of the universe. That today we can travel in space in no way diminishes the awe that the universe inspires in most of us. Likewise, all that is known today about psychology and how children develop in no way lessens our sense of the miraculous inherent in the growth of every human being.

Still, we have a body of knowledge about space travel that we use when undertaking it. We also have a body of knowledge pertinent to child-rearing that it makes equal sense to use when doing it. Granted, psychology is not a precise science in the way that physics tends to be—and every human being is unique. Yet there are *general principles* that apply to human development and human relationships, in spite of individual differences and regardless of circumstances.

This volume is a kind of over-view of certain significant principles—and ambiguities—that enter into guiding children from infancy into adulthood and relating constructively to them all along the line. It is intended to help parents to think through their long-range goals, to examine themselves and their attitudes, and to approach the job of being a parent with a certain amount of psychological sophistication. It deals with areas where the "rub" is likely to be especially discomfiting or challenging, and it attempts to indicate to parents how to use their knowledge of themselves, their children, psychology, and child development so that everybody *grows* through, rather than just suffers through, such experience.

It can not be stressed often enough that there is no magic recipe for rearing healthy children, and no one guaranteed right approach to any given challenge. Always parents have to weigh a number of variables—in the situation, the child, themselves, and, often, the larger society—and chart their own course, keeping in mind relevant guidelines. They are in a sense continually exploring new territory. This can add to the excitement of working with children, either as a parent or in other capacities. Nevertheless, just as we do not have to figure out the laws of navigation for ourselves, so we need not continually rediscover on our own all that is known about how people tick. There are always psychodynamic principles for parents to go on in handling the tasks they encounter. There are ways, to be examined here, of knowing more about what is transpiring in ourselves and in our children. Cultivating such awareness can lead to healthier parent-child interaction, help ensure the young the "watering" they require, and enable parents to grow as they nurture.

The impact of society on families and on the overall development of the children parents are charged with rearing is another matter that merits special emphasis. It is stressed at various points throughout this volume, but the author wishes that every reader would imagine every page to be headed by the following legend—in bold type: *"Parents are not solely responsible for how their children turn out."*

No single book can encompass all the information that might be helpful to parents. This book is issue-oriented and does not deal with the step-by-step pattern of children's development. There are times when familiarity with the master plan of growth can be invaluable to parents in determining what a child may be coping with, what kinds of behavior are to be expected within certain age limits, and how broad the range of "normal" development is at each stage. Parents seeking this kind of information to supplement the cues their own child gives as to what he needs will find some developmentally oriented books listed at the end of the Bibliography in this volume. The Bibliography also suggests materials on other subjects not covered here, or touched on only briefly.

Many people have helped with this book, directly and indirectly. Limitations of space prevent a listing of all publications consulted which the author found enlightening. Special thanks are due to Anna W. M. Wolf and Sidonie M. Gruenberg, long-time mentors; to my publishers, Edward Sand and Alexander Segal; to my editors, Patricia Ayres and Robert Doherty; and to my mother, my husband, and my children, who have served as excellent, although unwitting, teachers, as well as supplied the mix of understanding and *laissez-faire* that enabled this project to be undertaken.

1

The Expert In Each Of Us

WE HAVE ALL been children, had parents. We have seen the world through a child's eyes, listened with a child's ears, reacted with a child's feelings. Before we become mothers or fathers, the shoe is on the other foot for a long time.

This vast reservoir of firsthand knowledge about childhood and child-rearing that each of us brings to the job of being a parent can be one of our most valuable assets. But we have to learn to tap it with discrimination, alert to all it can tell us about the way children tick and mature, yet knowing the pitfalls sometimes associated with generalizing from personal experience.

Some parents make better use of their built-in expertise than others. We will explore this, mainly through the medium of parents' own words, with the objective of identifying factors that make the difference.

14

The Value of Empathy

One of the most important strengths that we can gain from having been a child is the ability to empathize with children, to sense how the shoe may be pinching. Few other skills serve a parent (or teacher) so well. Empathy involves correctly perceiving the emotions or thoughts of other persons and identifying with them. When we empathize with people, we feel what they are feeling, "know what they are thinking." In a family, this makes for mutual respect, rapport, a spirit of helpfulness and cooperation.

Empathy not only smooths everyday parent-child relationships but also gives rise to those "inspired" ideas, those "instinctive" right reactions that often enable parents to resolve vexing problems. A father recalls:

When our son went into second grade still unable to read, we were pretty uptight about it. Toward the middle of the year, his teacher suggested that I read aloud with him some primers she gave us and see if this might start him up. I did this several evenings in a row, until one night he said, "Daddy, I hate little words. I only like big words." It rang a bell with me. Since I'm a crossword puzzle fan, on the spur of the minute I said, "Okay, how'd you like to do today's crossword puzzle with me?" I thought he'd get bored quickly, but no. He even guessed a few words correctly. The next day I brought home a book of simple puzzles and we worked our way through them in a month or so. He may be the only kid in his class who learned to recognize "across" before "look" and "see," but by the end of the year he was reading well above grade level. He skipped the primers.

Flexibility Enters In

The point of the above incident is not that working crossword puzzles with children is a guaranteed way to teach them to read. As this father undoubtedly realizes, the number of nonreading seven-year-olds who are likely to stick around "helping" a father or a mother do the puzzle in the daily newspaper can probably be counted on one finger. Yet the father deserves credit for much more than astonishing good luck. His son's remark "rang a bell." Evidently it suggested to him that perhaps the way to help his child begin reading was to present the challenge in a more grown-up context, make it appear "harder." That's what the boy himself seemed to be asking for, and the father must have known, from personal experience or otherwise, that children are sometimes more responsive to "big" (adult) challenges than to "little" (childish) ones. The father empathized with his son at an important moment, coming up with what proved to be a very useful tactic. This is the message of the incident.

That crossword puzzles were, in this case, an appropriate challenge is probably due in large measure to the father's enthusiasm for them. Children enjoy sharing their parents' interests. Under different circumstances, "real" storybooks or the directions for putting together model ships might have been what worked. It should be noted that the father did not at first seize upon crossword puzzles as *the* solution to his son's problem. It was only after the boy showed surprising interest in staying with an activity that was over his head that the father saw the possibilities that simpler puzzles might offer. Operating in the father, along with empathy, are flexibility and sensitivity to the cues that a child gives.

Picking Up Cues

The mother of a three-year-old tells this story:

A while back I was having a terrible time with Margie. She was in a stage of saying "no" to everything. It really got to me. I began having this awful urge to smack her down, show her who's boss once and for all. And I'm not like that. My husband would say, "It's just a phase. Don't let her get your goat." But I couldn't help it. One day I was struggling to get her bathed and she kept breaking loose from me and climbing out of the tub, and I got furious and hit her really hard. She started yelling "No, no, no," and a weird thing happened. I remembered a time when I was little and screaming at my mother, "You can't make me." I don't remember what my mother was trying to make me do, but I could *feel* my determination never to give in, as if the whole thing were happening all over again. It stopped me cold. I hugged Margie and went into a spiel about how I didn't want to break her spirit. I'm sure she didn't understand, but something got through. She got back into the tub on her own. I can't say it's been all beer and skittles ever since, but there has been some kind of change in me. Her negativism doesn't infuriate me the way it used to do, and things seem a bit better.

Attitudes Can Change

Here, a mother's empathy is quite unexpectedly aroused during a highly charged encounter with her child. One minute she is threatened in her role as parent by her child's defiant behavior. She has a strong need to make her daughter acknowledge her as "boss." Then, suddenly, she remembers how being "bossed" feels to a child, and her attitude changes. She identifies with her daughter, which apparently makes it easier for her to gain the child's cooperation.

Regardless of whether the strong feelings that this young mother recalled, which changed her attitude, are the product of the incident in her childhood to which she ascribes them, or are the accumulated residue of many encounters that she has had with authority, she learned from them. She seems to have made a significant breakthrough in her relationship with her daughter, which ought to carry over into other relationships. She is starting to come to terms with her feelings about exercising authority, to see the problem as a matter of guiding and accepting guidance, rather than bossing and being bossed. Her statement, "I'm not like that," which for now has to be interpreted as "I don't want to be like that," may one day become literally true. Already she has used her memories of childhood to good advantage.

Using All We Know

In addition to giving us a capacity for empathy, our personal experience as a child leaves us with a great deal of specific information about how to cope with children in all kinds of situations. We should not underestimate its usefulness. Grandmother's knack for distracting us with an arresting question or suggestion when we were hell-bent on destruction is worthy of emulating. Some of her ideas may work the same magic with our children today that they formerly worked with us. In the back of our heads we carry around a treasure trove of knowledge about how to soothe, amuse, reassure a child, entertain him when he must be confined to bed, occupy him on a rainy day, help him learn new skills.

But the expert in each of us is not always to be trusted. We may misinterpret what various childhood experiences did for us—or to us. Our recollection of the past is spotty, at best. Time gets in its licks. Here or there we embroider, overlook or "forget" details that were extremely pertinent at the time. We may point the finger wrongly, or go to the other extreme and see events and people in a kindlier light than is psychologically defensible.

A very successful businessman, who grew up in a large, poverty-stricken farm family and worked his way through college, even sending money home all the time he was a student, says:

I've always felt I owe whatever success I've had to being able to work harder than most people and knowing the value of a nickel. My early life was no picnic, but the habits I learned then have put me where I am today. I wanted to teach my sons the same, for their own good. So they've earned their pocket money ever since they could push a lawnmower or wash a car. They've had paper routes, delivered groceries, the works. I thought it was all for the best, then my oldest was caught stealing from his last employer. The psychologist we've all been seeing since then put me onto something that never occurred to me. The way I grew up, everybody in the family had to work hard in order for us to survive. Believe me, I could always see how much my work was needed. That's certainly not true with my sons. I guess they're entitled to feel I'm stingy, though it hurts.

Blind Spots

This man, along with many other persons like him, mistakenly assumed that he succeeded in life *because* of his early deprivations, rather than in spite of them. His view of how children learn to value money and enjoy working is badly warped. His "teaching" was unrelated to the reality of his children's circumstances. He completely overlooked, until it was pointed out by his psychologist, what was undoubtedly one of the most important sources of the emotional strength that enabled him to overcome the handicap of grinding poverty: his feeling of being needed, of being able to contribute significantly to his family's welfare. In time, with the help that he is getting, he may be able to see why his sons need to feel needed, and find ways to give them this advantage.

All too often, parents tend to make virtues of the hardships that they survived as children, overlooking the positive factors in their experience that brought them through the hardships unscathed, or relatively unscathed. This may be why physical punishment is still viewed by some parents as "good for a child," rather than as one more example of children's capacity to weather parental imperfections as long as there is enough right in the picture.

Individual Differences

Another limit on the usefulness of our built-in expertise is the fact that it sometimes may not apply to our own children—or any other child. Often, the events from our past that we recall most vividly and accurately cannot teach us anything about anybody except ourself in a quite special environment at a particular moment in history. It is easy to overlook how different we all are, and what different worlds each of us lives in. It is especially easy to do this when we are members of the same family. All too frequently we fall into the same trap as Juan, who, when asked by his teacher what he had had for breakfast, responded, "Cream cheese and olives, like everybody else."

Always, we generalize from personal experience at our peril. The errors that this can lead us into may be, as in Juan's case, simply amusing and quickly discerned. One day, for example, discovering in an out-of-the-way drugstore a certain type of "penny candy" that we loved as a child, we stock up on it and return to our children expecting our find to elicit shouts of delight. What it elicits is more on the order of "You have to be kidding." On another occasion, we learn the hard way that the Disney nature movie we adored at ten is a flop with our son at that age. And so it goes.

Sometimes, however, the indiscriminate assumption that what was true of us when we were young will be true of our children produces results that are not

amusing. Many a child whose parents adored summer camp has been packed off lovingly to spend an expensive, miserable two months wishing he were back home knocking about with his dog or a kid down the block. Many a lifelong antipathy to classical music and concert-going has been established by well-meaning parents who sincerely wanted their children to "have the advantages I had."

Of course, the reverse is also true. Just because we hated camp at eleven is no reason to turn a deaf ear to Peggy's request to be allowed to go. And our disenchantment with violin lessons when we were eight does not warrant arbitrarily turning down Johnny's plea for them. Johnny at eight may not be "too young." He may just have real talent.

The Meaning of Projection

On a more subtle level, this same mechanism can occasionally lead parents to seriously misconstrue their children's behavior. A mother who was shy and rather lonely during her adolescence has this to say about her relationship with her teen-age daughter:

Soon after Elaine entered high school last year, I began to see a change in her. She seemed very tense and jumpy. She didn't talk much about the kids at school, and I figured she was having trouble making friends, especially boyfriends. As I had this problem at her age, I did all I could to reassure her, telling her about how I felt in high school, and later, and how people like us come into our own when we're older. Looking back, I realize she didn't open up much during these talks, but I thought we were as close as any other mother and daughter. I was shocked out of my mind when she got picked up on a drug charge recently. "Not Elaine," I kept saying to the officer. But it was true. Furthermore, all this time she's been going steady. That's how she started on drugs. Her boyfriend wanted her to keep him company. How could I have been so blind? I must seem terribly straight to her. I'm sorry about that, and I'm trying to treat her differently, but it's not easy. I'm worried crazy that she might get pregnant.

Examples of this sort represent a failure of empathy. Elaine's mother, and others who think that what held for them must hold for their children, are *projecting* rather than empathizing. When we project, we arbitrarily assign to another person characteristics, motives, and feelings that are ours, not theirs, overlooking the clues that they give us to understanding them as they really are.

It would be a mistake to conclude that Elaine's mother missed the mark because she is different from her daughter. Actually, the two probably have much more in common than they realize. Neither seems especially outgoing or at ease with people. But that is really beside the point. We don't have to be like a person, or have lived our life in a way that parallels his, in order to empathize with him. It can help, of course, but it is far from essential. Our common humanity—the fact that we have all known rage, fear, sorrow, embarrassment, love, delight—makes empathy possible under the most

24

unlikely circumstances. We can share laughter and tears with strangers. In a small shop in a foreign country where we do not speak the language, empathy gets our three-year-old whisked off in the nick of time to the proprietor's toilet.

Testing Our Expertise

So now we have two somewhat contradictory propositions. On the one hand, our experience as a child can help us in rearing children, give rise to empathy, brilliant problem-solving, breakthroughs in relationships, great ideas for things to do on a rainy day, and all that. On the other hand, we may sometimes be tempted by it into treating our children as if they were subject to the same wishes and pinches that we once were, which is not necessarily so. How do we make the most of our built-in expertise while avoiding the pitfalls that it may expose us to?

We can be alert to the chance that we might be projecting when we think we are empathizing. This possibility should certainly be checked out carefully when large issues—weightier matters than the choice of a casual treat or an afternoon's entertainment—are at stake.

For example, if Doug's fondness for a neighbor's dog makes his parents think of surprising him with a puppy on his birthday, they can check discreetly to discover whether the gift would indeed be as welcome as they suspect it might be. Is Doug ready for the responsibilities involved in caring for a dog? It may be that he enjoys playing with the neighbor's dog when he feels like it but doesn't really want one of his own for now. Or that if he is to be given a pet, he would choose hamsters. An offhand question or two asked at an opportune moment should bring out the information Doug's parents need to test their hunch thoroughly, without taking the edge off their planned surprise.

Granted, checking out our hunches is not always that easy. Elaine's mother faced a more demanding challenge. Communicating with adolescents can be tricky. They tend to resent anything that smacks of prying. Still, one feels that if Elaine's mother had not been so positive that she knew what her daughter was experiencing, if she had been less "blind" to her child's reactions, she would sooner or later have come closer to sensing the lay of the land. She would have given Elaine the opening that the girl apparently was looking for to confide in her mother and bring about meaningful communication.

We can be sensitive to the clues our children give us to what they are thinking and feeling. As the illustrations in this chapter suggest over and over, our child's behavior itself can provide us with one of our most reliable tests of the accuracy of our assumptions about him and the validity of our way of handling him in a given situation. From infancy on, he lets us know how well we are doing by him. When we make mistakes, as happens in the most empathic families, if we take our cues from our children, we tend to catch ourselves up quickly, before any great harm is done. A major goal all through this series is to help parents become better at perceiving and responding to all such cues.

We can be flexible. Of course, this enters into taking our cues from our children. Yet it is so important a quality that it deserves separate emphasis. Many psychiatrists and psychologists assert that flexibility is the key characteristic of the mentally healthy. (Others assign equal, or even greater, significance to the capacity for empathy.) We shall endeavor to help parents distinguish between being flexible and being wishy-washy or too tentative. We hope in various ways to encourage that combination of self-confidence and knowledgeability that enables parents to be decisive, yet able to shift gears, change course, roll with the punches, as circumstances warrant.

We can check our built-in expertise against authoritative source materials. If, for example, we feel strongly, on the basis of our memories of ourselves as a child, that unattractive personality traits, such as bossiness or being a poor loser, are more easily overcome if parents do not harp on them, it would still be wise to find out what professional investigators know about this. How are children best helped to outgrow these self-defeating ways of coping with life? Is criticism as unproductive as we remember its being?

It is a trifle inconvenient to whip off to the library every time you have questions of this sort, and do the research needed—wade through all the pertinent studies and case histories—in order to know what there is to know. Our goal is to present the latest information on child psychology and the principles of child-rearing in a way that will enable parents to inform themselves as easily and thoroughly as possible. Recognizing that young parents today are exposed to a steady barrage of advice about bringing up children, some of it conflicting, we always attempt to explain the "why" that lies behind any "how-to" offered here, so that you can make up your own mind about what to do.

We can work at acquiring a more mature perspective on our past. A young divorced mother, herself the child of divorced parents, tells this story about her relationship with her four-year-old daughter:

I remember how after my parents were divorced I hated being left with a sitter night after night while my mother went out on dates. I was determined not to put Susie through that. So for months after my divorce I lived for my child. We were together almost constantly. The only time I had a date or did anything on my own was when she was visiting her father, or friends, or her grandparents. She's quite a kid, but I must admit I missed not having a normal social life. Finally, I weakened and accepted an invitation to go to a party with an old friend. I was sure Susie would be upset when I told her, but she wasn't. You should have seen her excitement as she watched me get dressed up. She said, "I like to see you pretty." The next morning all she wanted to talk about was my party. I really think she enjoyed my going out as much as I did. It suddenly hit me that maybe I would have been even more unhappy after my parents' divorce if my mother had never dated. Who knows? I guess one extreme is as bad as the other.

Putting the past in proper perspective involves growth in understanding ourselves, a large and long-term task. As Susie's mother is discovering, there are seldom pat explanations for our feelings or behavior in a given situation. Nearly always, more is at work than is immediately apparent.

Aids to Growth in Self-understanding

Yet growth in self-understanding is possible. We can become more open to the multiplicity of factors that may affect the interaction between a person and his environment. Susie's mother now recognizes that she probably would have enjoyed, or at least accepted, her mother's dating if it hadn't been so frequent. She has discovered a useful concept: opposite extremes tend to be equally unsatisfactory. You will be introduced to many other psychological concepts that can help us make sense of our experience. In addition, parents will be encouraged all along, through firsthand accounts of experiences with children and other means, to examine themselves, to look for ways in which unrecognized attitudes or psychologically untenable opinions might be adversely affecting their children's behavior.

In passing, it should be noted that this kind of learning often comes through the arts. A novel, play, poem, painting, dance, music can give us insights into human nature and the human condition, stretch us. The "shock of recognition," or what the psychiatrist Fritz Perls has called the "Aha!" reaction, which marks psychological growth, is often part of the reward that we get from artistic experiences.

Of course, the furthering of growth in self-understanding is at the heart of all mental health education and all therapy. It is important to recognize that we can get professional help with the job when we need it. Such help can be extremely useful, as has been discov-

ered by the self-made businessman, mentioned earlier, who was having difficulties with his sons. However, one needs to be careful to seek help from qualified sources.

Professional Resources

There are a variety of professional persons and organizations equipped to help individuals and families understand themselves and their problems better: psychiatrists, psychoanalysts, psychologists, and social workers; trained and accredited counselors and therapists who work with specific problems, such as those involving learning or speech; mental health clinics, child guidance clinics, family service associations, and other public and private hospital-related, church-related, and university-related facilities that treat families and individuals and are often less expensive than private therapists. See the Bibliography for sources of more information about therapists, therapy, and how to go about getting such help.

It is a sign of strength to be able to seek out such aid when one reaches the limits of one's own resources for understanding and coping with what is happening to oneself or one's children. The need for professional help has always exceeded its availability. In recent years the burgeoning demand—swelled partly by persons who can function adequately enough but want more out of life, persons who feel they are overly inhibited—has led to the development of many shortcut approaches to self-understanding and self-realization: sensitivity training, encounter groups, marathons, touch groups, and the like. These approaches vary both in their potential for helping participants and their potential for harming the psychologically vulnerable who are unaware that they need professional therapy and not just to be "opened up."

The new movement has undoubtedly had a constructive effect on the overall practice of therapy. It has caused many traditionally trained therapists to adapt some of the new techniques to their purposes and to seek less time-consuming approaches to treatment.

However, the person interested in participating in any type of crash program aimed at heightening self-awareness and the ability to relate to others should be alert to the possible dangers involved. What are the credentials of the leader? What are the credentials of the sponsoring agency, if any? Are the participants carefully screened to eliminate persons with serious problems who might go to pieces during or after such an emotionally charged experience? Is there any professional follow-up; that is, are participants given the name of a trained person who can be reached quickly if one of them should feel especially depressed or disturbed after the experience?

Some people report that they benefited greatly from such experiences. Others report no gain. A few participants have become psychotic or committed suicide not too long after the experience, indicating that it may have triggered more awareness than they could handle without professional assistance. For the present, the crucial issue for would-be joiners seems to be the arrangements the program provides to cope with participants who may become emotionally upset during or after the experience. If you have doubts about joining, don't. Seek out more traditional resources for help.

Knowing Our Limits

You might say that the "expert" in each of us is limited by the degree to which we are emotionally healthy. Yet emotional health itself is relative, as is discussed in Chapter 4. Even the healthiest of us have our blind spots; and people with problems in some areas may have significant strengths in others. Our inborn expertise should never be sold short. The trick is to check it out, always, in the specific ways suggested here.

2

The World
We
Live In

WE DO NOT REAR our children in a vacuum. Our influence on them, as well as our ability to provide for and protect them, is decisively limited by the larger society in which we live, by the jobs, housing, schools, and health care available to us, the conditions in the neighborhoods where we reside, and the overall contemporary scene.

This is nothing new. What *is* new is the broad-scale discontent with society today that is evident among parents in all segments of our population, the white majority as well as minority groups, the well-to-do no less than the poor. Rarely, if ever, has society offered so little comfort and support to such a large proportion of its families. Rarely, if ever, have its values been so seriously questioned. Parents not only feel repelled or threatened by much that they see around them, but also share a sense of powerlessness, of being helpless victims of conditions over which they have no control.

Yet it is our world. There is no use in simply knocking it. Like every generation of parents before us, we have to meet the challenges of our times as constructively as we can. More than most, however, we need to try to understand our society as it is and how we can best involve ourselves in working for necessary changes.

Sources of Discontent

Not too long ago, those of us who did not have to worry about where our next meal was coming from viewed the threat of nuclear holocaust as the ultimate menace with which we and our children had to live. Today we know that pollution may render the world uninhabitable.

Already some species of our native birds are becoming extinct; the accumulation of DDT in their bodies causes them to lay eggs with shells so fragile that they crack prematurely and no live young are hatched. As the environmentalists say, "Birds today. People tomorrow?"

Almost daily we learn of some new ecological disaster: another lake or stream or beach lost to pollution, another species of fish declared unsafe for human consumption, another suspected link between a variety of human illnesses and the contaminated air that we breathe or the contaminated earth in which we grow our crops. And every day the population of the United States swells by 6,000 persons. By the year 2000, if present growth patterns persist, our population will be double what it was in 1950, heralding the prospect of mounting pollution; increasingly crowded schools, highways, and public transportation systems; more "brown-

outs"; longer lines at check-out counters; less speedy
mail delivery—you name it.

Meanwhile, nuclear weapons continue to be stock-
piled. As our supply of these and other implements of
destruction mounts, some inevitably become outmoded.
We are treated to the black comedy of government of-
ficials searching frantically for a safe way to bury, dump,
or otherwise dispose of antiquated war matériel—nerve
gas and the like—which, though obsolete, still has a
destructive capacity at which the imagination boggles.

Often we feel that our leaders, on the community
and the national level, are, like ourselves, helpless to
control the institutions that exert such a pervasive influence over our lives. The local school system, no less
than the military-industrial complex, frequently seems
to function under a momentum of its own that renders
it unresponsive even to the will of those in charge of it,
much less the average citizen. Bureaucracy has got the
better of us all, or so we often feel. It is easy to succumb
to the belief that we are all simply numbers, being fed
into computers and dealt with impersonally by the
machinery of our technology, because precisely this does
happen to many, possibly most, of us from time to time.
Without doubt, our sense of self—of feeling that we
have a voice, that we count for something—is increasingly being threatened, just as our physical person is
increasingly in jeopardy when we walk the streets.

The Need to Become Involved

There is good reason to believe that we must, as
never before, play an active role in the larger society.
If our children are to inherit a livable environment, an

aroused citizenry will have to effect changes in some areas very quickly. Time is running out. In regard to the ecological crisis, at least, we can no longer afford to "leave it to George," or "wait until the children are grown."

But what can or should we do? Granted, solving social problems is never simple. There are always conflicting interests to be reconciled. At a conference on technology, reported recently in *The New York Times*, space engineers in attendance were often asked, "If we can go to the moon, why can't we solve some of our pressing problems on earth?" The engineers continually countered that solutions to social ills are "not as neat and straightforward as developing a space-flight system."

Still, as the Chinese proverb has it, every long journey begins with a step. We must start where we can, perhaps in such limited ways as taking part in local programs to recycle bottles, aluminum containers, and paper, or joining a political club or a community group working for better schools or parks, better medical services, or improved relations with minority groups. In most communities today, if we look around carefully, we can find at least one organization striving to do a job that strikes us as "our thing." If not, we can start one.

Doing Our Homework

In the past, "volunteer" efforts to bring about social change have often foundered for lack of "professionalism." The volunteers did not inform themselves sufficiently well about the problem—education, recreation, housing, or whatever it happened to be—

that they had banded together to tackle. They did not know enough about the situation to set appropriate goals and gain the community support needed to achieve them. Or, being inexperienced in community work, they gave in too quickly to cynicism or despair. Or being unsophisticated about the psychology of groups—the interpersonal tensions and conflicts that are likely to arise and the ways of handling them—they became so split by internal disagreements that they could not function.

Parents who wish to engage effectively in work of this sort need to do their homework. Some suggested reading about several current issues, community action techniques, and the dynamics of group functioning is included in the Bibliography.

Learning from the Young

Today we are beginning to see a new, more professional breed of volunteers—willing and able to educate themselves about the job they are undertaking, not easily discouraged or distracted, psychologically aware. To a considerable extent, young people deserve credit for the change. As was first indicated on a large scale during the presidential primaries of 1968, when the youth of today volunteer for a job, they can exhibit a capacity for thoroughness, organization, and mastering the necessary know-how that puts many a paid professional to shame. It has become an axiom among civic leaders that if you want to get a project moving, interest some young people in it.

The head of an organization set up in a small Southern city to combat air pollution said recently:

We weren't getting anywhere until one of our members showed up at a meeting with his son, a high school senior, and two of the boy's friends. Within a few weeks the kids had come up with an impressive survey of industrial pollutants in our area, peak hours for pollution, weather conditions that might cause hazardous fallout, that sort of stuff. They suggested that we send out a daily release, "The Chemicals You Breathe Today," to our local newspaper. They assured us they could do the necessary analysis in the school laboratory under the supervision of one of the science teachers. Largely as a result of this, the Chamber of Commerce is showing an interest in our crusade. I'm afraid it will still be a while before we manage to get a satisfactory, enforceable Clean Air Code, but I'm in this fight to stay. I don't see how any of us could look our children in the eye otherwise.

Hidden Dividends

Implicit in this man's comment is a truth that all of us need to be aware of: though our efforts to change the world—or some small part of it—may not accomplish a great deal immediately, just being involved is good for us, as well as for our children.

A sound psychological case can be made for the importance of involvement to a person's emotional welfare, especially in today's world. In a society that is becoming increasingly depersonalized, our sense of identity is in danger of being eroded. It is easy to feel that we have no voice, that what we do does not matter. The next step is to feel that we do not matter as a person.

38

This can result in pathological depression or in paranoid rage, as Albert Camus' novel *The Stranger* chillingly depicts. Working closely with others in enterprises designed to bring about needed changes in the world provides an antidote to the malaise that afflicted Camus' "hero." It restores our sense of mattering, our identity. This is why the experience is so often felt to be rewarding, even though the impact of our efforts on the larger society may seem to us to be limited. We all need what involvement does for us, perhaps more than we realize.

A mother who lives with her husband and children in an apartment in a large city reports:

> We decided a couple of years ago to organize the tenants in our building to bring pressure on the landlord to lock the front entrance and install a bell-buzzer intercom system. We held meetings in our apartment and negotiated with the landlord and worked at getting tenants to agree to reasonable rent increases to cover the cost. A whole frustrating year elapsed between our first tenants' meeting and the day when the new lock and the new intercom system were finally working. During that year, I often thought, "Who needs it?" Then, after we achieved our goal, I began to appreciate all the other things we had accomplished in the process. The building is cleaner—we don't just leave everything to the super. We're like neighbors now, not intrusive but available when needed. I feel better about all those hours spent as tenants' representative than about any paid job I've ever had, and I think it's one of the best lessons our

children have ever been exposed to—you know, nothing is easy, but cooperation does produce results, tangible and intangible, if you keep at it.

A psychiatrist says this:

Originally, I went along with the recycling thing because of my son's feelings. Hands across the generation gap. Obviously, one family's trash is nothing. It's what the institutions do that counts, the hospitals, the restaurants, the manufacturers. I still say that's where the big battle has to be waged. But the first time we drove up to the receiving center with our two cartons of laboriously washed bottles and flattened cans, it came over me how important a symbolic act can be for the participants. All those beautiful people. If you're feeling down, I recommend a trip to your local recycling center.

Similarly, our children gain indirectly, as well as directly, from our efforts to make the world more livable for all its inhabitants. Our concern about getting better schools, for example, conveys to them, among other things, the message that education is important and reinforces their motivation to learn. Our work in a community project serving underprivileged youngsters says that we care about *all* children, and thus subtly reassures our own offspring that we value them as individuals, not as mere extensions of ourselves. Our involvement in community enterprises with people of other races and backgrounds takes the strangeness out of such differences; this makes the world seem less threatening

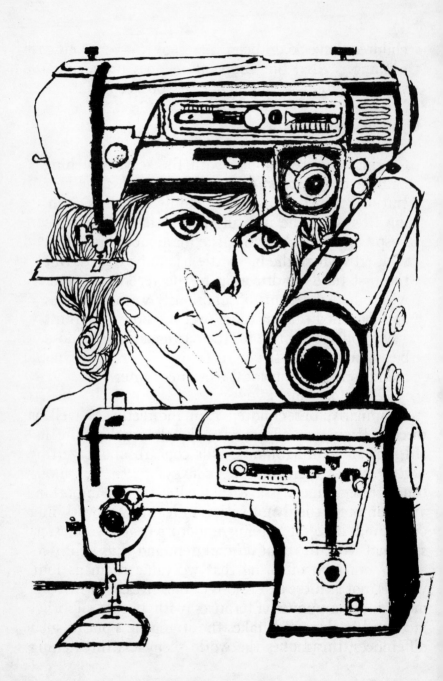

to our children. So, too, does the fact that we *work* with the problems that they are exposed to by television and the conversation of their elders.

Other Challenges of the Times

But, while we are working for social change, we must live in the world as it is and help our children do so. Of course, every family, like every child, is different. The problems that will confront us as parents will vary according to where we live, our economic situation, family background, and personal life-style. Still, certain general conclusions can be drawn about living in today's world that will, to a greater or lesser degree, apply to us all.

We will need to accept rapid change, be open to new ideas and new solutions. Most sociologists and other observers of the social scene agree that the tempo of change today is more rapid than at any time in recorded history, including the period of the industrial revolution, and that we should expect the tempo to continue to quicken. This means that our experience with living, especially with technological living, will become outdated very rapidly. We will have to work increasingly hard at keeping up with the times.

A mother in her early thirties had a taste of this when she decided to replace the sewing machine that she had owned for about fifteen years:

It was a real shock to my system. The new models they showed me were all so different from the machine I'm used to that I didn't see how I'd be able to thread one, much less run it. I felt so confused that I couldn't concentrate on what the sales-woman was showing me. I was ready to leave without buying anything when it struck me that I'm too young to start thinking that way. I was acting my grandmother's age. So I bought the simplest model, and I'm getting used to it gradually.

If you have recently replaced some of your old hi-fi equipment or investigated buying a "better" camera, you may sympathize with this young woman. In the same way, some of our ideas about children and growing up will tend to date faster. Young people who graduated from high school only five years ago report that already they feel rather strange with the current generation of high school students, so much has changed since their day. This doesn't mean, of course, that our own experience will lose its relevance; it means only that we will have to be continually alert to the significance of changing customs and social mores.

Today, for example, the parents of children entering first grade must reckon with the fact that their youngsters need to be informed about the kinds of drug experimentation prevalent among the very young. Many parents are as troubled by this as their own parents were by the need to let their children know that at school they would be likely to hear sex talked about in language they had not encountered at home. Since the days of Socrates, at least, many parents have clung to the delusion that what they don't tell the young can't hurt them, whereas communicating honestly about ticklish subjects is the best hope that adults have of protecting the younger generation from destructive behavior and of influencing their choices. Parent-child communication is dealt with more fully in Chapter 7 of this book.

If we are to make any real progress in alleviating the grave social ills of today, such as the drug problem, poverty, discrimination, pollution, the widespread dissatisfaction with our schools, and the widespread disillusionment with our national priorities, we must be open to new ideas and approaches. In a period of rapid change such as ours, young people—whose nature it is to see the world freshly—can be helpful in the search for new solutions if ways can be found to further cooperation between them and their elders.

We cannot foresee what specific conditions we may have to cope with, as citizens and as parents, in the decades to come. But we can school ourselves to be aware of the changing scene, to remain flexible, and to maintain meaningful contact with the young in our rapidly changing world.

We will confront new relationships between men and women. One social change that will almost surely continue in the years ahead will be the shift, so much in evidence today, in society's attitudes toward women and in women's thinking about their own role. Predicting the future is always hazardous, but it appears fairly certain that, perhaps largely as a result of the population explosion and improved methods of birth control, childbearing and child-rearing will cease to be viewed as woman's major function in life. Women may be expected to move steadily toward achieving equal status with men in access to professional education, employment opportunities, pay, politics, and many other areas.

Although many young women today express distaste or scorn for the "women's liberation" movement as such, it is interesting that nearly all will follow up their objections to the views and tactics of the more radical feminists with some such comment as, "Of course I believe in equal pay for equal work," or, "Certainly if a woman wants to go to medical school and has the qualifications, she should be judged on the same basis as male applicants," or, "I think it's ridiculous for a woman to be barred from a professional organization or a club just because she is a woman."

This heightened consciousness of their status seems to be shared by growing numbers of women in all strata of society. A mother in her forties reports that, in the course of doing research for an article about the educational experience of girls at the high school level, she changed from being rather opposed to the idea of women's liberation into being an outspoken advocate of women's rights. She says she had simply not been aware of, in her words, "the many subtle ways in which girls are brainwashed." Her husband, who shares her current views, remarks wryly, "But I could have told her." As more women—and men—come to feel similarly, the impact on society is bound to be far-reaching.

We will need to find new ways to recapture genuine community spirit. Ours is a mobile society. This lends a certain excitement to living, but we pay a price for it. Most of us in the course of our lives will call a number of places home, some so briefly that a decade later we would have difficulty finding our way back to them. Even if we stay put, our neighbors and our neighborhood change. Our relatives are more apt to be scattered at some distance from us than living nearby. Our children attend school with other children whose parents are, more often than not, strangers to us, and in going to and from school they are unlikely to encounter adults who have known and taken an interest in them since they were born.

There is less and less opportunity for most children to establish significant relationships with adults other than their parents. Likewise, parents tend to be more than ever left to their own devices in making important decisions about their children's upbringing, in dealing with emergencies, or just in coping with the daily exigencies of living. It used to be routine for neighborhoods to "look out for their own"—of all ages, but especially the young. Children were accustomed to being comforted, protected, advised, and admonished by a variety of familiar adults, which both contributed to their emotional security and broadened their horizons. It was a boon to parents, too, despite justifiable parental resentment against having neighbors meddle in their affairs. But this is now a rarity.

Today many young people in their late teens and early twenties are aware of the disadvantages of growing up in the kind of isolated "nuclear family" unit that is prevalent nowadays, in which children are dependent entirely on their parents for "parenting." These young people are experimenting with various ways to approximate the earlier "extended family." Their approaches range from communes to more casual cooperative arrangements for sharing child-care responsibilities and being neighborly. An excellent discussion of this trend can be found in *Parents and Teen-agers:*

Getting Through to Each Other by Margaret Albrecht.

The decentralization movement and the rise of tenants' groups and block associations in some urban areas may also contribute toward reviving a spirit of community. We cannot turn back the clock. Mobility, like technology, is here to stay. However, it must again become possible for neighbors to make common cause in various ways, and for neighborhoods to provide, even for those who settle in them only temporarily, the kind of expanded experience of "home" that they once offered.

We will have to face the possibility that our children may be more vulnerable than previous generations to pressures from their peers. As our children grow, they increasingly need to feel accepted in the world beyond home. Such acceptance is crucial to a child's concept of himself—his "identity." Much as he values his parents' good opinion of him, this alone is not sufficient reassurance that he is somebody. He seeks approval from others, especially his own age mates.

If a child's relationship with his parents is good, he tends, on the whole, to choose friends who share his family's values. Many other factors, however, will influence his choice of friends and his relationship with them at any given time. Though some youngsters seem to have a greater need than others to be accepted by their peers, and are therefore more vulnerable to pressures to "go along with the crowd," no child is totally immune to such pressures at every stage in his growing up. A quarrel with a best friend, difficulties with school work, reemergence of old rivalries with a brother or sister, any one of a myriad such stresses can intensify a youngster's need to be "in" with certain peers, or peer groups, and affect the lengths to which he is willing to go to achieve this reassurance.

In earlier times, youngsters usually gained considerable sense of status through "belonging" in a community where they and their family had lived for years. This contributed to their identity, reducing their need to win recognition in other ways and often easing the path to lasting friendships. The fact that such close community ties seldom exist today puts a premium, for many children, on the ability to relate to peers. Peer pressures may be harder to resist.

We will need to recognize that children are growing up faster these days. The average age of puberty, for both boys and girls, has been gradually lowering over the last few decades. Intellectually, too, youngsters tend to be ahead of where their parents were at the same age, judging by the change in scores on a variety of standardized tests. If you have looked recently at a teen-ager's school books and assignments, you probably don't need to be told this.

Improved nutrition has been credited by some authorities with bringing about earlier physical maturation, although nobody knows for sure why the age of puberty is falling or where it will stop. The information explosion and, especially, television contribute to the intellectual sophistication of today's children. Although television programming can be faulted on a number of grounds, and although television watching can become an escape mechanism, somewhat like a drug, the educational impact of TV on many young viewers has been enormous. Possibly, the current concern over the gap between the American dream and the American way of life is the result of television, although the programmers never intended their shows and commercials to produce this result.

To say that children are growing up faster does not, of course, tell us anything about a particular child. We have always had our early and our late maturers, our delayed "bloomers," children who were precociously sophisticated and those who were the opposite. The range of individual differences remains as broad as ever. As parents, we will be relating to a human being who does things at his or her own pace, not to a nonexistent statistical average. Still, we have to recognize that statistical averages affect the overall climate of the world in which our own child is growing up. Awareness of that climate makes us better able to help our child deal with it wisely, in the way that is right for him.

We will increasingly be required to make our own judgments about the flood of information reaching us as parents and citizens. The information explosion, combined with "instant communication," will continue to step up our exposure to varying viewpoints and seemingly conflicting "facts" about matters that directly concern families but cannot be authoritatively checked out with a specialist, such as the family doctor. When specialists disagree (as they do, for example, about the relative safety of the artificial sweetener saccharine, or the merits of breast-feeding), we must decide for ourselves what is the most sensible course for us to pursue. We will have to accustom ourselves to evaluating evidence, weighing alternatives, and reading the fine print on everything.

This might turn out to be all to the good. From having to pick our way through the morass of information relevant to living in today's world, we may recapture the self-reliance, the independence of spirit, and the feeling of being able to cope with our environment that earlier generations of Americans acquired through pioneering in the wilderness. That would be no mean gain.

We need to view new threats and dangers in proper perspective. We should not overlook the fact that significant progress has been made in some very important areas in this century. Life expectancy has risen from 49.2 years in 1900 to 70.2 years in 1970. The infant mortality rate has been cut by a third since 1930, dropping from approximately 65 deaths under one year per 1,000 live births to 22 per 1,000 in 1968. During the same period, maternal mortality has been cut from approximately 7 maternal deaths per 1,000 live births to less than 1. Medical advances have given us new drugs and vaccines that can protect us and our children against many diseases that were intensely feared only a few decades ago: pneumonia, scarlet fever, measles, polio, to name a few. Surgery has become correspondingly safer. And technology, for all its faults, has relieved us of many of the more burdensome aspects of running a home and rearing children. Although such gains have not been shared equally by all citizens, they are not to be dismissed lightly.

These facts do not minimize the threats that confront us today or the unknown ones that may confront us tomorrow. They merely put them in perspective. Pollution, violence in the streets, and all the rest must be faced up to realistically. While we work at identifying and treating their root causes, we must educate our children to avoid whatever hazards it may be within a child's power to avoid. Youngsters must, for example, be given pointers on navigating as safely as possible within their neighborhoods and environs. It may be helpful, to them and to us, to frame our teachings within the context that the world has always had its dangers and imperfections, and always will.

We will have to learn to live with more stress. Even if we manage within the next decade to stabilize the population, there will still be a lot more of us around by then, making for a lot more frustration.

There is nothing new about trains running late, mail being lost, banks making mistakes, or most other examples of institutional fallibility and/or technological breakdown that are the source of so much irritation today. Such frustrations have simply multiplied with the population explosion. To complicate matters, machines handle many large-scale operations today, and machines are, on the whole, sadly lacking in the ability to catch themselves up when they make an error.

A young father recently had his wallet stolen. The wallet contained his driver's license, which was very important to him, as his job required considerable traveling by car. He immediately notified the authorities and was informed that no record could be found of his ever having had a license, possibly because such records were in the process of being shifted from one type of machine to a newer model. However, he was assured cheerfully, if he were indeed a licensed driver, sometime before the end of the year he would automatically receive a renewal application, so that if he could afford to wait, all would probably turn out well. He could not afford to wait. It was suggested, then, that he apply for another license. This he did. In due time, the forms for renewing his earlier license arrived, as predicted, and he had to spend the better part of two days consulting with the authorities about which license he should keep, it being against the law in his state to have two.

This may seem an extreme story, yet nearly every day most of us hear from our friends and families similarly unnerving accounts of hours wasted coping with bureaucratic red tape, or inaccurate bills—or simply trying to get from one place to another.

Although some young people are trying to avoid these extreme contemporary pressures by setting up more primitive societies in isolated areas—in rural New England or the mountains of Tennessee or Colorado, or on the West Coast—for most of us there is no "getting away from it all."

Nor are there any magic recipes for living with modern stresses. A sense of humor, being able to laugh things off, helps. But one does not acquire that ability just by wanting to have it. On the other hand, some psychiatrists insist that we tend to become what we go through the motions of being. If this theory is true—and there is evidence to support it—then it might be helpful to cultivate the habit of joking about the frustrating dilemmas from which we can not extricate ourselves. Jokes are known to be a psychologically useful way of letting off steam.

Certainly, parents can sustain their children

through frustrating experiences, such as being caught in
a traffic jam or waiting in a clinic, by making light of
the situation—if it is quite clear that they empathize
with the child's feelings. It is important that children
not feel alone in their frustrations, or think that they
are being laughed at, rather than with.

Often, too, our children can help us through stressful times, take our minds off our troubles. Since they
are not always affected as we are by all the ramifications
of a situation, their reactions can be fresh and cheering.
A three-year-old, flying with her parents during a violent
storm that was severely frightening most of the passengers, greeted each "bump" that the plane encountered with the happy squeal that she often gave when
sliding down her backyard slide. Eventually one of the
male passengers smiled weakly and remarked, "That
child has to have been sired by a dive bomber." A few
neighbors laughed. Soon, many of the passengers became so interested in the little girl and so intent on
shielding her from their anxiety about the plane's
safety, that they themselves felt better. The trip took
on something of a carnival quality.

Parents sometimes, in various ways, let themselves
in for more than the necessary amount of frustration
and stress. A common way is through trying to "keep
up with the Joneses." At best, bills tend to pile up during the early years of marriage, when husbands are just
getting started in their work, and the presence of small
children limits the ability of wives to augment the
family income. However, persistent financial problems
are often a signal that we need to rethink our values
carefully and consider the possibility that our priorities

should be reordered. Other attitudes that may subject us to potentially avoidable stress will be discussed from time to time in succeeding chapters.

It's Not All Up to Parents

A promising development in recent years has been the growing recognition that parents are not solely responsible for how their children turn out. Society shares that responsibility all along. Children, too, share in shaping their own destiny. Increasingly as they grow, they move into the community and make decisions that vitally affect their lives. The new view of child-rearing as an undertaking in which society, parents, and the child himself are all partners eases some of the pressure on parents and underscores the need for commitment to social change in high places. Although some families and some children are more victimized than others by the social problems of the day, we are all vulnerable to the ills of our times. No child is assured of having a healthy environment to grow up in until all children are.

It is not helpful to our children, to ourselves, or to society either to be prophets of doom, or to give up trying to change the world in which we live. Children do not thrive on a constant diet of pessimism or apathy. They need to see that we share their questions and concerns about conditions around us, to understand that many other parents feel as we do, and to believe that society can be changed to better meet the needs of all its members.

3

Preparing For a New Baby

Nᴏᴛ ᴇᴠᴇʀʏ ᴄᴏᴜᴘʟᴇ is overjoyed when they realize they are going to have a baby. For some, of course, the event is urgently desired, perhaps long awaited, and as suspicion gives way to certainty, they walk with their heads in the clouds.

But others are annoyed—they would like to have children eventually, but not right now. Right now they have other fish to fry, and the coming of a baby is going to play hob with their plans. In the case of some, annoyance is too mild a word for the emotions engendered. They are enraged, or frightened. They simply cannot afford a baby, they think, or afford housing that would provide space enough for a baby, or their marriage is foundering, or the husband is about to be transferred to a job in a distant city, or the wife has just one more year to go to get her degree in medicine or social work or something.

Feelings Can Change

Often, couples who were resentful or worried at the start of a pregnancy come around to being delighted long before the baby is due. Together they hash out their feelings, go over the choices open to them, change some plans, rearrange some of their long-term goals, and gradually the future begins to look bright again, maybe even brighter than before.

A young mother of two children says:

I was so upset when I got pregnant with my second child that I considered having an abortion. My husband had quit his job the year before to go back to school and get his law degree, and I was working. He wasn't happy about my getting pregnant just then, but he dragged his feet about abortion. We stewed and argued for about a month, then things began to fall into place. His old company agreed to take him back and pay his tuition to finish law school at night. He'll graduate next spring, and our girl has been the apple of our eye ever since the day she was born.

As this mother's experience suggests, negative feelings about a pregnancy need not mean that you will be an unloving parent later on, or that your baby will be in any way adversely affected by the fact that for a period of your pregnancy you were prey to grave misgivings and doubts. Such feelings are extremely common. In fact, few prospective parents escape having *some* doubts somewhere along the line.

Talking Out Feelings

You shouldn't feel guilty about your negative feelings. The important thing is to talk them out. Pregnancy is a time when it is especially necessary that husband and wife be honest with each other, admit to each other their inmost thoughts and emotions. In sharing their private hopes, fears, and dreams about having a baby, each partner may discover new sides of his own personality, as well as his mate's. Self-doubts, never before admitted, may at last come out in the open, along with hidden ambitions, unexpected strengths, and unexpected tenderness and compassion for each other. There is opportunity for growth as a person, growth in marriage, and growth in one's relationship with one's own parents.

Dr. Paul Adams, a child psychiatrist, writes in a paper included in the book *Children's Rights:*

Pregnancy . . . constitutes a kind of turning point in the relationship of the man and woman. Wonderment, joy, anger and irritation may all appear, presenting new opportunities for dialogue, for compromise and for self-assertion by both partners. A cosmic concern appears fleetingly even to the most blasé of young couples. They begin taking cognizance of their own origin . . . begin showing a preoccupation with their own parents. . . . It is as if they desired to set aright the relations with those generations which preceded them just at that moment when their own generativity comes to the forefront.

Women especially are apt to find that becoming pregnant puts them on a new footing with their parents, their mother in particular. But men also may experience this. Even more than marriage or the first "real" job, knowing that one is going to have a baby makes a young person feel, "Now I am an adult." Parents, too, feel a difference. There is often a new ring of respect in the way they react with their children. Young people, on their part, may find themselves turning to their parents for advice—and taking it. The generations may become truly equals. When this happens, the closeness that it brings can provide a prospective parent with an additional, exceedingly valuable resource for talking through all his or her concerns, and often supply a tonic that has been missing: humor.

Serious Doubts

Sometimes talking out negative feelings doesn't cause them to diminish. The more husband and wife discuss the matter, the clearer it becomes that, for one reason or another, both of them are seriously distressed by the pregnancy. Both wish intensely that it had not happened.

In such cases, it would be wise for them to think about a legal abortion. Information about abortion and resources for securing it legally are given in Chapter 10. Through the tenth week of pregnancy, that is, up to about the point when a woman is missing her third period, a legal abortion is both very simple and very safe. After that it becomes more complicated, though still safe, through about the twentieth week. After the twenty-fourth week, abortion can no longer be performed legally. So this is a decision that should be made early. However, a couple has several weeks of leeway, after they first suspect the wife is pregnant, to think carefully about the possibility of having an abortion, arrive at a decision, and make plans before the wife is ten weeks pregnant.

Of course, for some couples abortion is out of the question. They reject it absolutely, on religious or other grounds. For them, some kind of professional counseling would seem advisable. A clergyman trained as a pastoral counselor or a psychologist or psychiatric social worker who shares their convictions may be able to help them with their anxieties about having a baby.

Couples who feel a conflict, who want an abortion but fear they may have guilt feelings about it later, would also be well advised to seek professional help in making their decision. Talking with the family doctor may be sufficient. If additional counseling is desired, the doctor can suggest where to go for it. The evidence suggests that guilt feelings about abortion are related to the climate of opinion to which a woman is exposed. Women in countries where abortion has been legal for some time and is taken for granted do not seem to be subject to guilt feelings after having an abortion.

Choosing an Obstetrician and Hospital

Good prenatal care is important to the welfare of both a mother and her unborn baby. Most obstetricians and prenatal clinics prefer to see a mother as soon as she has missed her second period. By this time, pregnancy can be confirmed or ruled out with a high degree of certainty. On the first visit, the mother's overall health is checked, and she is given some general instructions, often in writing, about diet and other matters to guide her throughout her pregnancy. She also is given the opportunity to ask any questions she may have on her mind. After the first visit, she returns for regular checkups, usually at monthly intervals.

Most women today live in areas where they have a choice of physicians and, often, hospitals. Perhaps you have already decided what doctor you want, or in what hospital you prefer to be delivered. If you have chosen a doctor, you will automatically be booked for the hospital where he practices. If choice of hospital is crucial to you for some reason—perhaps because it permits "rooming-in" (discussed on p. 70) or is receptive to "natural childbirth" (discussed on p. 71)—you can either use that hospital's prenatal clinic or call and ask for a list of staff obstetricians engaged in private practice.

If you know nothing about doctors or hospitals in the area where you reside, you can call your city or county Medical Society and ask them to recommend an obstetrician or a prenatal clinic. You will be given several names. Every person needs to know this, in the event he faces a medical emergency in a strange community. But perhaps you consider it too impersonal a way to choose your obstetrician. You want to go to a doctor recommended by somebody you know. In that case, you might ask a clergyman for recommendations, or a neighbor whose judgment you trust, or your husband might ask advice of his boss. Personal recommendations, when the source is reliable, are always worth having. Another possibility is to contact a doctor in another area whom you or your parents know well and ask him for a referral. Although he may not personally know a physician in your area, he has resources for finding a reliable person and may supply you with a note of introduction.

Technically, an obstetrician is a doctor certified by the medical profession as a specialist in obstetrics (delivering babies) and gynecology (problems related to the functioning of a woman's reproductive system). He has had advanced training in his specialty, passed certain examinations, and of course had a great deal of experience in the practice of obstetrics and gynecology. However, the term obstetrician is often loosely used to refer to any doctor who supervises prenatal care and delivers babies. General practitioners usually accept pregnant patients, and there is no reason not to feel thoroughly comfortable about putting yourself into the hands of one who has a large obstetrical practice. But if you prefer a specialist, check to see that the doctor of your choice is certified in obstetrics and gynecology. Ordinarily he will have a framed certificate attesting to this fact hanging on the wall along with his medical degree.

One final caution: On your first visit to your doctor or prenatal clinic, you will be warned against taking any medication, including aspirin, unless specifically prescribed. This is a very important rule that should go into effect at the beginning of pregnancy, even before you see your doctor. We have long known that some viral diseases, such as German measles, and some drugs, such as the tranquilizer Thalidomide (now banned), can damage a mother's unborn baby, especially during the first six weeks of pregnancy. Today, other viruses and medications are also considered suspect. It is wise not to take chances.

How Will You Feed Your Baby?

Whether to breast-feed or to use a bottle is a decision that husband and wife should make together. The hundreds of studies that have been made comparing breast-fed and bottle-fed children add up to one fact: It is not the method chosen, but how the feeding situation is handled, that matters. Babies need to be cuddled attentively when they are fed, by someone responsive to the cues they give about how the feeding is going, when they need to be burped, and when they have had enough. This can be accomplished with either breast-feeding or bottle-feeding. A woman should feel free to choose the method that appeals most to her and to her husband.

Doctors sometimes have rather strong opinions about which method is preferable. They may dwell on the advantages of one over the other. If you don't happen to agree with your doctor, tell him so. A good physician will respect a mother's decision on this subject. Most doctors recognize that a mother's feelings about how she wants to feed her baby are influential in determining the success with which she handles this crucial aspect of infant and baby care. Of course, if your doctor has a valid medical reason, in your particular case, for ruling out one method, accept his judgment. Remember that your baby will thrive whichever method you use.

If you are going to breast-feed, you should begin to prepare your breasts during pregnancy. Your doctor may offer suggestions. In addition, it would be wise to read up on breast-feeding, so that you will know what to expect during your hospital stay and during the early weeks after you return home with your infant. Consult the Bibliography for recommended sources.

Where Will the Baby Sleep?

Not all couples have an extra bedroom waiting to be turned into a nursery. If space is at a premium, parents may feel that the easiest solution would be to have the baby share their sleeping quarters. However, since a great deal of advice to parents warns against doing this, they may have qualms about it.

The only drawbacks to this arrangement for the first two years of a child's life involve the effects that his presence may have on his parents. Babies are restless, "noisy" sleepers. Having one in the room with you may seriously interfere with your getting a good night's rest. Additionally, parents may find that the arrangement is not conducive to their leading a healthy sexual life. After a child is two, the setup has potential hazards for him. It is generally agreed that a child as young as two can be emotionally disturbed by overhearing his parents' sexual activities, and children of this age are not always asleep when you think they are. Also, having his parents in the same room with him continually may be sexually stimulating. Inevitably, it tempts the child to try to climb into bed with his parents, which is not advisable.

So by the time your child is two, you should arrange for him to sleep apart from you, and you may want to do this from the start, or at least before he becomes habituated to your presence in the room. Is there a part of a hallway, a corner of the kitchen, or other space capable of being screened or curtained off to accommodate the baby's crib? Babies and young children are not disturbed by diffused light or the noise of normal family activities. In fact, they may sleep the better for both, especially if they grow up accustomed to them. Another possibility, of course, is for parents to give their child their bedroom and sleep on a convertible couch or folding bed elsewhere.

Choosing a Doctor for Your Baby

The concept of the "family doctor," a physician who handles all the medical problems of the families who are his patients, from delivering babies to treating sore throats, may be undergoing something of a revival —and high time, many people believe. Most women today, however, are likely to have their babies delivered by one doctor and looked after by another. If you plan to use some sort of a well-baby clinic, you will not need a private doctor for your baby. Otherwise, this is a choice that should be made a month or so before the baby is due to be born.

Ideally, your baby's doctor should examine your infant while he is still in the hospital, be involved in any recommendations about feeding or special care that the hospital gives you, and be available to answer any questions you have about the baby during the early weeks. When your baby is approximately six weeks old, you will take him to the doctor's office, or to your clinic, for the first of many regular checkups.

Any doctor who treats babies and children is often

loosely referred to as a pediatrician. Technically, the term applies only to doctors who have had advanced training in this specialty and been certified by the American Board of Pediatrics. If you want such a specialist, check for this credential.

The suggestions offered earlier about choosing an obstetrician apply in general to picking a doctor for your baby. Since the relationship between parents and their pediatrician tends to be especially close, it is important to have a physician whose views about child-rearing you feel you would share on the whole. This can be determined through talking with other parents who have used the doctor.

Planning for a Mother's Return from the Hospital

For the first two or three weeks after a mother returns home with her infant, she will need full-time help with running the house and caring for her baby. Husbands have been known to take their vacation during this period and give wives the assistance they need. This often works out extremely well for all concerned. But if a husband is poor at housework or dislikes doing it, and especially if both husband and wife are inexperienced at handling a new baby and a bit nervous about the prospect, other arrangements will need to be made.

Many women want their mothers with them at this time. Mothers, mothers-in-law, and other relatives who have had experience handling an infant may be just the answer, if they offer their services. Since this is a period when emotions run high for the new mother, and often her husband as well, care must be taken to have help from a person with whom both husband

and wife, and especially the wife, believe they will feel comfortable. A member of the family is usually, but not always, most likely to meet this requirement. The couple need a fairly calm person who is willing to do things their way and not insist on imposing her ideas about housekeeping or infant care. They require support, not bossing. Under some circumstances it may be wiser to go to the expense of hiring help rather than accept it from a relative.

On the whole, mothers usually prefer to care for their infants while somebody else sees to the housework. In interviewing a prospective employee or weighing a relative's offer of help, you will need to ascertain whether the person is willing to do the "dirty work" and leave the mother mostly free to feed and bathe her baby and to rest. You don't have to have a practical nurse, and so-called baby nurses often will not do housework. Friends, your doctor, or your prenatal clinic may recommend a competent person or sources for obtaining appropriate help.

You should make suitable arrangements for help several months before the baby is due to be born. Whatever arrangements you make, you may also want to look into the possibility that you may be eligible for help from your local Visiting Nurse Service. The nurse would come only briefly once or twice a week, but she might offer reassurance that things are going well, and she would be able to answer any questions that you might hesitate to bother your baby's doctor with.

If a husband foresees having to be away overnight during the first two or three weeks after his wife's return from the hospital, this factor needs to be taken into account in arranging for her help. It is unwise that she be left without another adult in the home (or readily available nearby) for more than a very few hours at a stretch.

Husband and Wife as a Team

A young couple expecting the birth of their baby imminently chanced to overhear—as they strolled down the street clad alike in jeans and workshirts and with their hair of similar length—some conversation behind them regarding the erosion of sex distinctions. The young wife swung about suddenly and said with a grin, "Pregnancy lets the cat out of the bag."

It does, in more than just the obvious way. Many young couples today achieve in marriage a degree of sharing that is enormously satisfying to them and quite touching to observe. Either partner is capable of supporting the other financially, and over the course of the years they may take turns at this from time to time, to enable each to function optimally as a person. Either partner can soothe a crying infant, explain mathematical set theory to a fourth-grader, do the shopping at the local supermarket, prepare the evening meal, and correctly identify—and use—a socket wrench. But not every role, as yet, can be exchanged, and not every couple is dedicated to "sharing equally."

There are still men in their twenties who don't want to cook, change diapers, or be with their wives in a hospital labor room. In a pinch, they may *have* to do the first two chores—and hopefully will come through as gracefully as strong men have for generations. But there is no need for them to do the third if they really don't wish it.

We live in an age when both men and women should feel freer than ever before to be themselves. It would be a pity to limit this freedom by arbitrarily expecting every member of the "now" generation to share certain interests and characteristics. A couple awaiting the birth of their baby need to discuss honestly how they want to share baby care, household tasks, and all their other responsibilities. Frankness is essential to finding ways to accommodate the individual needs of both partners. Conflicts need to be brought out in the open and explored, so that reasonable compromises can be reached.

During the pregnancy a husband may be surprised, perhaps dismayed, to discover that his wife, who hitherto seemed quite competent and able to look out for herself, can be moody, demanding, "unreasonable." Pregnancy affects the emotions, as well as the body. This is caused by hormonal changes and the reality of the woman's situation. Having a baby may make her feel dependent upon others to a degree that she has not experienced since early childhood, and these dependency feelings can be hard for her to handle. Occasionally she may need to "test" the strength of her husband's devotion, much as a child sometimes tests his parents. Understanding this may help husbands to be more sympathetic. The problem is transitory. Soon after delivery, a woman usually becomes her normal competent self, often with more energy than either she or her husband knew before that she was capable of.

Wives, too, need to be sensitive to the fact that the prospect of having a baby subjects a man to emotional strains. He may feel not only that his powers as a breadwinner will be tried, but also that his standing with his wife is in some danger. They are no longer going to "mean everything to each other." The fluctuating emotional needs of both prospective parents will challenge their ability to continue communicating frankly and to support each other as partners in marriage, equal but somewhat different.

A Word About Equipment

The temptation to buy more baby equipment than is really necessary, and to spend more on necessary items than is required, is very strong, particularly when a couple are having their first child. This is sometimes sadly true of couples who can least afford it.

Of course, having a few pretty things for special occasions is fun. Life would be unbearably drab if we were always "sensible." However, the "fun" items often turn up as presents, so it is wise to go easy in this area at the start.

Baby garments made of machine-washable knits and other easy-care fabrics are one of the great boons of contemporary civilization. (Ask any grandmother.) They are often brightly colored and designed to make dressing the baby easy, rather than a chore. Sleeping garments will do duty around the clock in the early months, and you will need no more than three or four. A machine-washable sweater or two will be useful even in summer, except in very hot climates. As any friend who has recently had a baby will tell you, watch out for purchasing garments too small.

Many mothers find fitted crib sheets a convenience. If you plan to make your own crib sheets from worn bed linen, you may want to give them fitted corners. Good crib blankets can also be made by cutting down larger-size blankets that are worn in spots.

If you are going to wash the diapers yourself, you had better have at least three dozen. The fitted ones are easier to use, as they do not require folding, but they are sized and will be outgrown from time to time. If you would like to use a diaper service but don't feel that you can afford it, you might ask grandparents to consider treating you to this in lieu of some other present. Some mothers swear by disposable diapers. They find it is easier and no more expensive to use them than to use a diaper service.

It is on the large items of equipment that very substantial savings are possible. Thrift shops and Salvation Army stores offer bargains in used cribs and carriages (if hand-me-downs are not available), which often can be refurbished so that they look practically new. These are good places, too, to pick up a chest for the baby's belongings. Choose a chest that is the right height to serve as a dressing table when topped with a folded blanket or mattress pad (or, if you sew, a tailor-made cover).

A baby can be bathed in a kitchen sink lined with a bath towel for protection. However, inexpensive plastic tubs, in a variety of colors, are available.

More information about equipment is supplied in sources listed in the Bibliography. It is always helpful, too, to talk this over with other couples who have recently become parents, bearing in mind, of course, that your definition of "necessary" may differ from theirs.

Doing Your Homework

You will have a lot more time for reading before the baby comes than after. Now is the time to bone up on what is in store for you. In addition to reading and discussing the material in this volume, prospective parents are advised to read a book such as *Three Years to Grow* by Sara D. Gilbert. If this will not be your first child, read a book such as *Primer for Parents of Preschoolers* by Edith G. Neisser for information on preparing older children for the arrival of a new baby.

"Rooming-in"

Some hospitals have facilities that permit the infant to stay in the same room with the mother, instead of in the hospital nursery. That is, they approximate what used to happen almost universally a hundred years ago and still does in primitive societies. The infant's crib can be rolled within easy reach of the mother's bed so that from the beginning she can comfort and feed him, play with him as often and for as long as it suits them both, and, in general, attend to all his wants, though a nurse can be summoned if the mother wishes assistance.

Rooming-in appeals to some mothers. They find it reassuring to know just what is going on with their infant at all times. If they are breast-feeding, they may especially like the freedom to feed "on demand" that this arrangement affords.

With rooming-in, visitors are limited usually to the husband and one other person—no substitutes allowed. This is considered necessary to protect the infant's health and the mother's emotional equilibrium.

If, after carefully weighing all the pros and cons, a woman decides that rooming-in is for her, her doctor will need to make reservations well ahead of time at a hospital that offers the service. The couple will have to select an obstetrician who is on the staff of such a hospital. In other words, their choice of doctor will be circumscribed by their choice of hospital.

"Natural Childbirth"

The concept of "natural childbirth" developed out of the conviction of a number of doctors that pain during childbirth is largely the result of fear; that if a woman understands how her body functions during the birth process, she will be unafraid, able to relax when that is desirable and to push when needed, and thereby to deliver her baby with a minimum of medication and of discomfort. Various authorities have devised exercises for the purpose of preparing a woman to function more effectively during childbirth. How one breathes during labor contractions is considered especially important, and breathing exercises are a major part of all such programs.

If you are interested in natural childbirth, talk it over with your obstetrician. You will need his approval in order to enroll in any formal exercise program. If you merely want to read one of the available books on natural childbirth and do the recommended exercises informally at home, your doctor is unlikely to have any objections, but it would be wise to discuss it with him anyway. Two such books are listed in the Bibliography.

When the natural childbirth movement first started, some mothers were so fanatical about rejecting

all medication that the whole concept fell into disrepute
with many doctors. Recent books on the subject, however, handle the question of medication more sensibly.
If you are going to try natural childbirth, trust your
doctor's judgment about what medication is needed
and when. He has to think ahead. As one mother said,
"When my doctor ordered a Demerol shot, I assured
him I didn't need it. Half an hour later, just as the shot
started to take effect, I was grateful for his foresight."

Understanding what goes on during childbirth is
helpful to any woman, as is confirmed by many mothers
who, in their words, "want all the medication I can get."
Labor is a rhythmical process. The uterine muscles con-
tract forcefully for about a minute and then relax for
a period of time. The contractions come closer together
as labor progresses, but between them many women
experience no pain whatever. Lying on one's side during contractions and puffing out one's abdomen, by
taking a big breath and holding it until the contraction
ends, may alleviate discomfort.

During the first stage of labor, which is much the
longest, the cervix dilates sufficiently to let the baby
through. (See illustration.) For the first few hours of
this stage, a woman feels little, if any, discomfort. The
only way in which she can facilitate the dilating process
is by relaxing during contractions. She can be given
some pain-relieving drugs, but not too much medication.
Doctors do not want to deliver a drugged baby. The last
half hour or so of the first stage of labor is generally
the most uncomfortable part of having a baby. So it is
consoling to know, when you are going through it, that
soon the worst will be over.

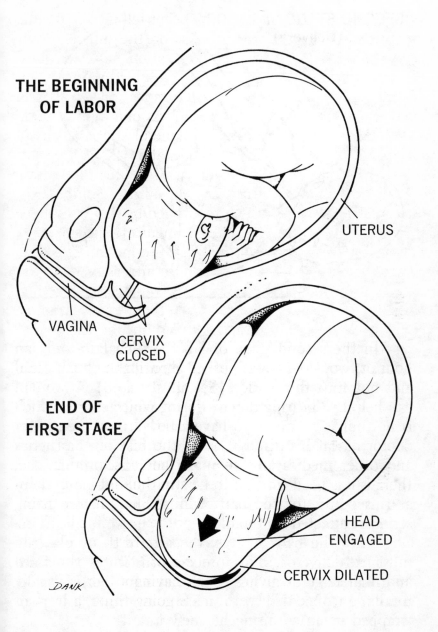

THE BEGINNING OF LABOR

UTERUS

VAGINA

CERVIX CLOSED

END OF FIRST STAGE

HEAD ENGAGED

CERVIX DILATED

DANK

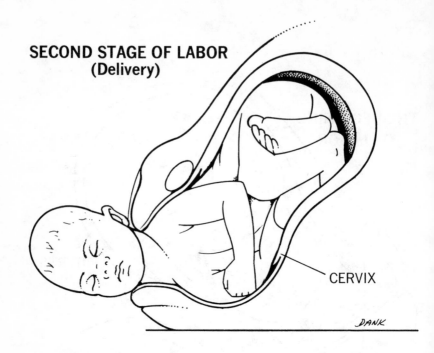

SECOND STAGE OF LABOR
(Delivery)

CERVIX

DANK

In the second stage of labor, which lasts only an hour or two, the baby is pushed through the birth canal and out into the world. (See illustration.) A woman can help by "bearing down" during contractions, which is not unlike straining to have a bowel movement. Her doctor has at his disposal a wide variety of anesthetics and other medications to make her comfortable, and there is less need for him to be stingy about using them at this point, for the baby will be born before being seriously affected by them.

After the baby arrives, the afterbirth or placenta must be delivered. This process constitutes the third and final stage of giving birth, and a mother is usually totally unconcerned with it. She is either asleep or wrapped up in admiring her new infant.

"Mother Love"

Since the perfection of spinal anesthesia, which blocks out all sensation in the pelvic area without putting a person to sleep, any woman can enjoy what is extolled as one of the greatest benefits of natural childbirth: she can be wide awake when her baby is born. Not every woman wants this, however. If you do not want to watch your baby being delivered and would prefer to wait to see him until after he has been all cleaned up, tell your doctor. Ordinarily, he will discuss with you, early in your pregnancy, what kinds of medication he might administer. He should be able to put you to sleep at the time of delivery if you prefer that.

Every mother is different. There is no reason to feel that not wanting to see your baby born implies that you might lack normal maternal feelings.

Mothers (and fathers) react differently also to the first sight of their newborn infant. A newborn is, at best, not pretty, except possibly to his own parents. The head of the newborn is likely to be rather startlingly pushed out of shape—elongated—by the birth process. (It will round out in a few days.) The legs seem pitifully thin and bowed. (They will straighten and plump out in a few months.) The infant's facial features are "scrunched together," giving him the appearance of an old man, and the skin is wrinkled and often blotchy. (That, too, will be soon remedied.) All in all, it is surprising that any new mother or father should consider their newborn beautiful, but some do.

But probably the most unsettling thing that happens to some new mothers is the discovery that they are not overwhelmed with maternal feelings when they first hold their baby. Many women are, but not all, and this tells nothing about their capacity to be good mothers, or how much they will love their child later on.

In many mothers, and fathers, love for their child develops slowly, through ministering to the baby's needs and watching him grow into "a person." Some excellent mothers admit that they really do not care for infants at all. They did not begin to come into their own until their babies started to coo and gurgle at sight of them. Still others say the magic moment came even later, after the child began to walk and talk.

Some Goals to Keep in Mind

As you plan for the coming of your baby and make all the many decisions that this involves, here are a few general guidelines that may stand you in good stead:

Try to keep your options open. This means having alternative plans to choose from, remaining as flexible as possible. For example, it's the rare baby who arrives exactly on schedule. Most come a week or two before or after the estimated due date, and some are even earlier or later than that. That time factor must be taken into account in arranging the initial help that a mother will have and deciding other matters. Remember, too, that after the baby is born you may see some things differently from the way you see them now.

Don't expect too much of yourself. If you don't get around to painting the kitchen or the baby's chest before he comes home, he will never notice. Pregnancy is a good time to start learning how to cut corners judiciously, as you will need to do a lot of it when you have an infant to care for.

Watch your priorities. It is more important for a woman to get the rest and relaxation she needs during pregnancy than to keep her home in apple-pie order. Money spent on an unnecessary frill for the baby might be better used for groceries, so that the mother-to-be has the nutritious diet that she needs. Whether it is a matter of finances or work to be done, husband and wife need always to set their priorities thoughtfully, asking themselves what is truly essential, what is less so, and what might be dispensed with.

Trust your judgment. In the days and years ahead you are going to be exposed over and over again to conflicting advice and pressures. It will be up to you to decide how you want to do things, after weighing the available evidence. This doesn't mean that advice should not be listened to. Quite the contrary. Your maiden aunt Sue may have a point. In any case, she deserves a courteous hearing. But you must decide how you will lead your life and rear your children.

Of course, when parents are young and inexperienced, they are often prey to doubts: "Maybe I should have listened to my mother, instead of to the doctor, about when to start the baby on cereal; Pat's baby is so much bigger than mine." You will have to remind yourself that however carefully you inform yourself, however intelligently you evaluate the sources of your information, you will inevitably experience some regrets, have some bad moments. But even infants are remarkably hardy little creatures. In time you will feel more secure about doing things your way.

4

No Parent Is Perfect

WE ALL MAKE mistakes, sometimes from lack of knowledge or experience, sometimes simply because we are human. "If only I had known about demand feeding when my children were infants," a mother says wistfully. Another mother regrets that she did not play with her first baby more and pick him up when he cried. With her second child, she had sufficient courage to find out for herself that such treatment does not cause "spoiling." Still another young woman wishes daily for more patience. She does not believe in physical punishment, but when she becomes angry she occasionally hits her children and finds it hard to forgive herself afterward.

Unavoidable Hardships

Then there are all the hardships and heartaches from which we are powerless to protect our children:

78

painful surgery; an unsympathetic teacher; death in the family; the "unfairness" with which nature sometimes parcels out ability among brothers and sisters; budgets that will not allow for that special toy, or outfit, or experience that even the least demanding child occasionally sets his heart on; danger in the streets; living in a neighborhood that offers no really safe place for children to play and encourages precocious sophistication —all the "slings and arrows of outrageous fortune."

Life Is Like That

In this chapter we will offer parents a framework, based on the latest thinking about mental health, in which to view their limitations and their children's difficulties realistically, without undue guilt or anxiety, but without undue complacency either. As we shall see, children do not require perfection. They can adjust to the fact that their parents are fallible and, in the process, learn something about human nature and about living. Given adequate support, they can withstand even severe hardships—those experiences that it is not within our power to spare them—and still turn out well.

For several decades now, the pressure has been on parents to a degree that does nobody any good. We shall look at some historical and other roots of this excessive pressure. We shall also consider some recent psychological findings that may help parents face their job with more equanimity; to see it as a long-range enterprise during which, though things go wrong from time to time, there will be many "second chances" to help their children and themselves acquire the strengths that make for emotional health.

Our Role

One reason parents often feel more guilt than they should is that our society tends to blame parents, quite unfairly, for all their children's problems. If a child has trouble adjusting at school, or lands in juvenile court, or exhibits any other kind of problem behavior, it is commonly assumed that the fault lies with his parents. "They must have done something wrong," is the usual reaction. Few people stop to wonder what the school, or society, might have done differently. Almost nobody considers the possibility that the parents are doing the best job possible under the circumstances and that the problem results from a multitude of factors over which they have little or no control.

It cannot be repeated too often that parents are not solely responsible for how their children turn out. The nature of the society in which families live—employment opportunities, the quality of housing, education, and health care available, neighborhood conditions, the climate of the times—all these factors crucially affect what happens to children, just as they crucially affect the lives of parents. Also, children are not equally easy to rear. Each presents a highly individualized challenge, which may vary in degree of difficulty from time to time. And each, as he grows, is increasingly responsible for making the decisions that determine the course of his life.

This is not to imply that we should stop blaming parents only to start blaming society or the child. Assigning blame is, at best, an unproductive activity. We need to be aware of all the complexities involved in rearing healthy children in contemporary society, and to seek new ways in which families can assist each other and society can give to both parents and children the support needed to minimize their problems overall and help them through crises when they arise. What is required is planning not only for more mental health clinics but also for a more livable world.

Children's Vulnerability in Perspective

Another source of excessive parental guilt and anxiety is the failure of the general public to appreciate children's ability to withstand stress. This failure has roots in history. Early in the century, when psychoanalysis was giving us new and profound insights into human functioning, it was rather commonly assumed that an individual's problems as an adult could be traced back to a childhood trauma, or emotionally disturbing experience, usually involving his relations with his parents. Though this idea that a single traumatic event will inevitably scar a child for life has now been discarded, many parents still are frightened. They worry about every move they make, every frustration that their child is forced to endure, fearful that one false step or trying event might somehow spell disaster.

We now know that an individual is affected by all that he experiences, both outside and within the family over a period of many years. There are repeated opportunities for him to outgrow problem behavior, with or without the help of others. It is the long-run, broad-range picture that matters, the sum total of all that he is exposed to. The occasional "mistakes" that all parents make are weighed in with everything that we, and others, manage to do right over the years.

82

Children are capable of successfully weathering severe shocks, such as the death of both parents, and even prolonged stress, such as that engendered by physical disability or poverty, if there are enough positive factors in the picture. Conscientious attention from some trusted adult does seem to be necessary all along the line, but an interested teacher, community worker, relative, or other parent substitute, including a brother or sister, may alternately fill this role at various stages of a child's development, as is attested to by the biographies of a number of well-known persons.

Toward a New Definition of Mental Health

Until recently, nearly all of our knowledge about emotional functioning was derived from the study of persons who had problems severe enough to require hospitalization or cause the person to seek psychological help. An enormous body of useful information has been acquired in this way, but, not surprisingly, as it filtered down to parents, it tended to make them extremely sensitive to all the things that could go wrong, and by extension, all that they might "do wrong." Since, in addition, it was widely assumed that an emotionally healthy person was one who had no clinically identifiable psychological problems, child-rearing came to be viewed as fraught with a staggering assortment of potential pitfalls.

One can, certainly, gain valuable insights into what makes people emotionally healthy through understanding the problems of those who are not. Today, however, a fresh wind is blowing in the mental health field. A number of psychiatrists, psychologists, and others in related professions have been acting on the hunch that it would prove fruitful to study persons who have never sought psychological help and are considered emotionally healthy by those who know them well. So far, this view through the other end of the binoculars has shown that the persons who pass for healthy among their peers are not without problems in a clinician's eyes. Their childhood histories indicate that they tended to have as many, and in some cases more, serious difficulties than a sampling of persons who have needed therapy of some kind at some point in their lives. What distinguishes the emotionally healthy persons is their ability to keep going in spite of their problems, to fight through their difficulties, whatever they happen to be, and eventually grow out of them.

We cannot as yet (and may never be able to) pinpoint precisely what it is that enables some people to cope successfully with the emotional difficulties that all of us have from time to time, while others either break down or require professional help in order to keep functioning adequately. In psychological circles, the phrase often used to sum up this critical quality is *ego strength*. Psychological theory has it that the *ego* controls conscious behavior, in contrast to the *id*, the instinctual drives that come with us into the world, and the *superego*, the "conscience" that we acquire as we grow up. The id and the superego are at work mostly in "unconscious" behavior—slips of the tongue, for example, or a man's erection, or the risking of our lives in a rescue effort. Ego strength implies the capacity to reconcile the often conflicting interests of the id and the superego and to do whatever will enable the person to function in a way that best serves the totality of his needs. From the layman's standpoint, a wide variety of strengths, such as self-confidence, flexibility, joyousness, and determination, appear to be involved. The healthy person does not necessarily have *all* the strengths mentioned. In fact, one alone may be sufficient to get him through a bad time. For example, a child who early acquires the feeling that he is somehow special may throughout life retain enough confidence in his powers so that he can come through difficulties that would be devastating to a person less sure of himself. Another individual may manage to weather his problems because he has a special talent for enjoying whatever there is to enjoy in life. He (or she) is the person who, even when his world is threatening to crash around him, will respond with delight to a spring morning, a child's laughter, an invitation to a party.

Using Our Leeway Prudently

When mental health is seen as being relative, and as having to do with strengths rather than the sum of our weaknesses, it becomes clear that parents have considerable leeway in which to operate safely. We need not feel that we are walking a tightrope. The journey is going to be a long one, and we will have many opportunities to help our children make the most of their potential.

Problem behavior is, of course, always a problem for the child and for his parents. It calls for intelligent attention from parents. If, for example, a seven-year-old boy, who is normally fairly easy to live with, becomes tense and irritable at home and bridles at everything his parents say to him, we do not dismiss his behavior lightly, assuming that he is simply going through a "phase" of some kind. He may be, but we would want to find out what is occurring in his life outside the home that might be causing the problem. Is he having trouble at school, with the work or with his classmates? Has he become as touchy with his friends as with his parents? What interests or strengths does he have that we might draw upon in order to help him feel better about himself and relate better to us? Can we arrange for more fun things for him to do, with us, or with others?

Often parents know right away what is causing a child's difficulties. In fact, they may have been expecting problem behavior to appear. The coming of a new baby, for example, or a stay in a hospital, a move to a new home, and many other such potentially stressful experiences are often accompanied by problem behavior. Given time and sympathetic understanding (not to be interpreted as suspension of sensible parental controls), the child tends to outgrow problems brought on in this way.

Sometimes, however, parents are completely in the dark as to what could be upsetting their child. Problem behavior does not always have readily identifiable precipitating factors. If none are easily apparent, parents had best avoid worrying about what may have gone wrong and just assume that something is going on inside the child that is none of their business. Prying into a child's private feelings is never advisable, although, of course, one needs to be open to confidences if the child makes a move in that direction. Difficulties of this sort also tend to be outgrown in time when they are accorded the same common-sense sympathetic handling given more "understandable" episodes of problem behavior.

As long as a child continues to function adequately in most ways and to develop overall as children of his age should—that is, he does not markedly *regress*, become decidedly more babyish in every way—parents can afford to conclude that he will in time outgrow his difficulties.

However, if months pass without improvement, during which parents have done all they can to help their child find satisfactions in his daily living, then psychological help should be sought.

"Second Chances"

Children often develop personality traits that cause their parents concern. Personality seems to be the product of both inborn predisposition and the experiences to which a child is exposed. When an undesirable trait appears, it is not profitable to worry about what we might have done as parents to ward off this particular development. Probably nothing. But there is a great deal that we can do over the years to help our offspring grow out of personality limitations.

For example, the normal rivalry that exists between brothers and sisters often leads to one child's becoming unattractively bossy, or touchy about losing, or undesirably fearful about competing for fear of losing. It is well to remember that such traits can just as easily be acquired by a child who has no brothers or sisters. Sibling rivalry may call parents' attention forcibly to a child's personality disabilities, but, on the other hand, when such traits come to our attention early, we have

that much more opportunity to help our child modify his behavior.

The art of accomplishing this is a delicate one. Adult criticism is effective only if a child feels good about himself in general and if the criticism is worded sympathetically—"I know why you feel like behaving that way, but . . ." Humor helps, when it comes naturally. Even with young children, there is a limit to how often criticism should be repeated. Once the child gets the message, understands that we do not find his bossiness or some other aspect of his personality pleasing, the change that we desire will have to come out of his own wish to change. All we can do is continually provide him with evidence that we are an admirer of his.

Whether the change that parents hope to foster is relatively limited, such as helping a small child curb his bossiness, or more all-encompassing, such as encouraging a youngster to spread his wings and be less fearful about making mistakes, we are more likely to succeed if we direct our efforts generally toward helping the child feel pleased with himself and find life as satisfying as possible, rather than making a big issue of his shortcomings. As we will see in the following chapter, children can often be browbeaten or frightened into obeying the limits that we set on their behavior, at least when we are present, but real personality change occurs on a deeper level and is never brought about through punishment.

If, for example, we try to root out five-year-old Andy's tendency to boss by punishing him whenever he exhibits the tendency, his frustrated aggression is likely to show itself in some other problem behavior of an even more troubling kind. To become less bossy, Andy has to see himself as a competent little person, recognize that there are more attractive ways to get what he wants, and feel supported in the effort to handle his aggression acceptably, not feel simply that he is always prevented from having his way.

"Second chances" of all kinds may come early in childhood or much later. For example, the mother mentioned earlier, who feels that her oldest child was short-changed on attention during his first year, has found that as a preschooler he shows no signs of being the worse off for it. In the space of only a year or so, either his parents—more sure of themselves and of what small children need—have managed to give him whatever compensation he required in the way of extra patience and time in order to develop into a delightfully secure and inquisitive toddler, or other factors have combined to produce this result. On the other hand, another child who was handled similarly as a baby remained, much to his parents' chagrin, somewhat inhibited and cautious until adolescence, when suddenly he too blossomed. Whether the change is due solely to his parents' continuing efforts to bring him out, or whether it is at least in part the result of certain fortunate, rewarding experiences outside his family, nobody can say for sure. And it doesn't matter. Despite what both sets of parents now refer to as their shortcomings when their children were babies, the two children are doing well.

Learning from Mistakes

Parents are often understandably upset when they

come across material that convinces them that they erred in how they fed, or weaned, or toilet-trained their child. They may hesitate to read about rearing children younger than theirs presently are, for fear of discovering that they did something wrong.

But, as we have seen, mistakes can be corrected or compensated for, once we recognize them. Each day offers fresh opportunities to affect the long-range picture. A parent who is aware of the various stresses that his child may have been under in the past, whether avoidable or unavoidable, is in the best position to recognize and make good use of all his second chances. For example, a father who did not realize, when his son was four and five, how strained father-son relations often are at this age and why, may, as a result of reading about the preschooler's sexual development, make a special effort to go out to his preadolescent boy and have the patience and understanding needed to maintain a sound relationship with him during the difficult years of adolescence.

The fact that we do not always live up to our ideal of what a parent should be can also teach us, and our children, how to make do within our limits. Parents differ, of course, in how much they can take in the way of whining, or sibling baiting, or messiness, or noise, or lack of sleep, but we all have our limits. For each of us there comes the point when we have had it. The sooner we learn to recognize when that point is about to be reached, and what frustrations are most likely to move us toward it, the better we will be able to function within our limits.

A mother who knows, for example, that she is at

her worst on days when the weather keeps her children indoors might talk over the problem with her husband and friends and come up with some fresh ideas about handling the situation. Similarly, if there is a particular time of day when she is most prone to blow up, she can look into the possibility of rearranging the family's schedule with the hope of improving matters. If it is an aspect of the children's behavior, such as bickering, that triggers parental explosions, this can be talked over with the children. They may become better at keeping some of their disagreements out of parental earshot. They may also appreciate and learn to respect a timely warning, such as, "You know it gets on my nerves when you do that."

Knowing and trying to work within our limits in ways such as this will not accomplish wonders. Sometimes, however, it can improve the quality of daily living enough so that everybody feels a bit better about themselves.

Even explosions have their uses, if they are appropriately handled and do not become the major way of coming to terms in a family. They set the record straight about what each parent is like and can take. Nearly all parents, including those who do not believe in physical punishment, have occasionally hit their children in anger and done other things that they regretted. When parents can admit their regret to their children, say "I'm sorry," no lasting harm is done. Such incidents may clear the air and enable both parent and child to calm down and proceed more reasonably. The child realizes that even adults are fallible, that they lose their tempers and can be pushed into doing things that they do not really approve of. Knowing this may relieve the child of some of his guilt feelings about his own "bad behavior." A fitting apology assures the child of his parents' love and their respect for him as a person, however small or dependent on them he may be. It also drives home the importance of an apology, not only as a means of asking forgiveness of others and being restored to their good graces, but also as a way of forgiving ourselves for our failings. If we ask their pardon, children are generally quite touchingly quick to forgive us for mistakes made in the heat of anger.

Asking What We Should of Ourselves

We are entitled to be philosophical about our shortcomings and about the misfortunes from which we cannot protect our children, but they deserve the benefit of the strengths we have to offer. Knowing our strengths helps us to employ them well and also to see our weaknesses in perspective.

The fact that we take care of a child day after day, provide him with meals, clothing, and shelter, show concern for his welfare, monitor his comings and goings, is one such strength. Its importance is often underestimated by parents, and by children while they are growing up. The parents may wish that they had more money to spend on food, clothing, shelter, and recreation. If so, the child will certainly add to their frustration by asking for, or obviously wanting, things they cannot afford. And, since much of the friction that occurs in every family results from the fact that parents care enough about the child to monitor his comings and goings and other behavior, this, too, is rarely viewed by

either side as a blessing while it is going on.

Yet there is ample evidence that children not only need but also appreciate our routine efforts to look after them, and parents who do the best they can with the available money get full credit for this. Rules and regulations formulated with a child's best interests at heart may be disparaged and resisted, but they are nonetheless correctly perceived as signs of love. Our concern for our child and the elementary daily care that we provide continually contribute to the child's sense of security and his all-around emotional health.

But beyond this, a child has other needs that should

not be slighted. Parents can use their individual strengths in many ways in meeting their children's needs. Children need intellectual stimulation and enjoyable physical activities that help them become well coordinated, and they thrive on having fun with their parents. We always do a more effective job when we take into account what we do well and really like to do, along with the child's individual interests.

For example, a mother who is a great reader, and knows what exposure to books can do for children, discovered to her dismay that she intensely disliked her three-year-old's taste in books. When it became apparent that he felt the same way about hers, instead of dutifully rereading to him books that she detested, she fell back on an ancient device and asked if he would like her to tell him a story. He acquiesced. The first story, about a man shipwrecked on an uninhabited island, went over so well that it had many sequels. Storytelling came to be a popular accompaniment for mother and child while preparing meals, doing the laundry, even waiting in the doctor's office. By the time the boy entered school, his mother had delighted him with her freehand renditions of many of the classic adventure yarns and fairy tales. He had a large vocabulary, good attention span, and soon was reading facilely "for information," which was what interested him. He had been "intellectually stimulated," painlessly for all concerned, and apparently added to this his mother's enthusiasm for such activity. Quite beside the point, but worth mentioning, when the boy was twelve he came home from school one day and said to his mother with considerable consternation, "I guessed that some of those stories you used to tell me came out of real books, but I always thought you made up Robinson Crusoe."

As parents we have to be willing to extend ourselves frequently to meet our children's needs and further their overall development. Sometimes the challenge is cut and dried: a sick baby has to* be held or rocked; the request, "Will you test me on my spelling words?" calls for just that. Often, however, we have some choice in deciding how to meet various challenges, and in these instances the child gains more when we are truly enjoying what we are doing.

Making and Living with the "Hard" Decisions

In the course of rearing our children we will inevitably be called upon to make decisions that involve choosing the lesser of evils, or weighing the needs of one member of the family against those of another member or against the needs of the family unit. Making these decisions is among the more trying experiences that parents have to endure.

For example, if for financial reasons the mother of a young child is suddenly forced to seek employment, she will need to keep down the cost of having her child cared for while she is at work. It is likely that she will be unable to afford what she considers ideal arrangements. She must choose the arrangement that appears to have the fewest drawbacks for the child, for herself, and for the rest of the family and hope that she has correctly evaluated the pluses and minuses of every option open to her. Similarly, parents may have to weigh the advantages of a husband's accepting a better job, involving an impressive rise in both position and pay, against the disadvantages of having to move away from a city where their seven-year-old deaf child has many friends and is attending an excellent day school for the hard of hearing.

Nobody can tell us what our decisions should be in circumstances of this sort. There is no "right" choice. It is we who are in the best position to assess what price each possible course of action is likely to exact and what compensations each has to offer. We must be prepared for the fact that whatever our choice, we probably will not get home free. There will be regrets, second thoughts, times when we will have to eat our words. Occasionally, as with arranging for substitute parenting for a small child, we may find ourselves facing the same dilemma over and over again, with little to be learned from previous bad experiences except that our society does poorly by families in such straits. The best that can be hoped for is that when two parents are involved, they will provide emotional support for each other. Such support from a spouse, or relative, or close friend can make all the difference.

Once upon a time, nearly all parents rested secure in the conviction that, having made such difficult decisions to the best of their ability, the outcome was in the hands of God, who "read our hearts" and judged us by our efforts, not their results. This kind of assurance that one does one's best, then rolls with the punches, is enormously guilt-relieving and strength-providing. Here modern psychology joins hands with religion. We can do no more than our best for our children. Much is out of our hands. But doing our best should be, in itself, rewarding enough.

5

What Makes Johnny "Behave"?

W<small>HEN WE ARE</small> having trouble getting a child to take a bath, or leave his sister alone, or come to supper, or set out for school on time, or do any one of a thousand other things that we want him to do (with justification), we may tend to feel that discipline is all child-rearing is about. Everything else seems as nothing compared to the job of "making Johnny behave."

Discipline is indeed important. But it is a teaching process that encompasses a great deal more than policing a child's behavior. The core question is not "How do I make my child mind?" It is "What kind of person do I want to help my child become?" Only when we have our ultimate goals clearly in mind can we think discriminatingly about what limits to set on a child's behavior and how to enforce them.

Six major goals that need to be taken into account will be examined in this chapter: (1) keeping children

97

safe; (2) nurturing self-esteem; (3) inculcating respect for the rights of others; (4) encouraging growth toward independence; (5) the development of good "inner controls" (that is, the child's ability to regulate his own behavior); and (6) building healthy attitudes toward authority. We shall see how keeping these goals in mind can help a parent function more intelligently in setting and in enforcing limits. Finally, we shall discuss some of the thornier issues that parents always seem to want to talk about, issues such as "permissiveness" and punishment, and look into how they are related to the goals listed above.

Keeping Children Safe

First of all, of course, we need to keep our children alive and in one piece, so the child's safety is always a consideration of paramount importance. It governs the amount of weight that we can afford to give to other goals, such as encouraging independence. Usually it begins to figure in parents' thinking about discipline very early, about the time a child starts to creep or crawl rapidly.

Parents not only seek to keep their newly mobile baby safe, but generally at this point they begin trying to interest him in helping with the job by teaching him to avoid potential hazards to his safety: stoves, hot-water faucets, and all the rest. This teaching picks up momentum as the baby becomes a toddler. Since he will, as he grows, take on more and more responsibility for keeping himself out of harm's way, parental teaching about safety is of critical significance. We do not want to make our children overly fearful or timid, but they must have a healthy awareness of the dangers that exist in their world.

If we are too protective, the child may not develop the capacity to properly assess potential hazards and become skillful at avoiding or handling them. He may lose his drive to venture and explore, to trust his judgment and try his wings. Or he may rebel against the restrictions with which we hedge him about and grow deaf to all warnings. On the other hand, if we give him too much leeway and do not go to reasonable lengths to protect and instruct him, we invite trouble on two levels: he may seriously injure himself; and he may not acquire the respect for his person that every child needs to have.

From the very beginning, our efforts to keep our children safe tell them that we value them, and, by extension, this helps them value themselves and their physical well-being appropriately. Thus, while we are ensuring their safety, we are building their self-esteem. The correlation between these two factors is especially high and especially important during the first few years of life.

In addition to being realistic about danger and restricting our children enough but not too much, we have the job of helping them learn, at the appropriate time, how to handle certain potential hazards safely. The toddler who is prohibited from stepping off the curb alone will grow into the child who must be taught how to cross neighborhood streets and then busy intersections, and, finally, how to ride a bicycle in traffic. Sharp knives, matches, tools, a host of other useful equipment that he is initially forbidden to touch, he must eventually become skillful at using. Acquiring the skill he needs to be trusted with activities of this sort also contributes to a child's self-esteem and his growth toward independence.

Nurturing Self-esteem

Our approach to discipline affects a child's self-esteem in other ways. The manner in which we customarily enforce limits makes a difference here. If we are constantly harsh and punitive, show no respect for the child, he is unlikely to feel much respect for himself.

No child is too young to have his opinion and feelings respected, even when he must be prevented from acting upon them. Thus, a two-year-old bent on climbing the steps of the playground slide, or throwing sand at another toddler, or sampling the dog's dinner has to be stopped, of course. But he deserves to be given an explanation of why he is being stopped, not just yelled at or hit. After all, he is only doing what any two-year-old might do. We need to recognize this truth and somehow convey to him our awareness of it. He is not "bad," or "stupid," or "impossible to teach." He is simply a small child who has much to learn and needs a lot of patient help with doing it.

Many factors outside the realm of discipline also affect a child's self-esteem, notably the way in which feeding and weaning are handled and the overall quality of "mothering" a baby receives during his first year of life. However, the way in which limits are enforced exerts a continuing influence in this area, starting when parents first begin to "discipline" their children. Since genuine respect for the rights of others appears to grow out of esteeming oneself, it is desirable that a child's experiences during his early years contribute to building adequate self-esteem. Yet, parents always have the opportunity later on to help a child improve his opinion of himself. An understanding, nonpunitive approach to helping children operate within reasonable limits, however late parents get around to trying it, can do a great deal to heighten poor self-esteem.

Inculcating Respect for the Rights of Others

Parents actually begin much earlier than they may realize to help their child accept the need for limits. Even if they start out feeding their infant on demand, within a month or two they ease him into a more regular pattern of eating and sleeping, sometimes helping him wait a bit for a meal, sometimes rousing him for a feeding. This is the child's initial exposure to learning to adapt to other people's needs. Over the course of the first year, if the baby is sensitively handled—encouraged to make some adaptation, but protected, to the extent possible, against prolonged or severe frustration—he gradually becomes increasingly capable of accommodating himself to the needs of various members of the household. The groundwork is laid for him to accept many kinds of limits dictated by the fact that other people also have their rights.

During the preschool years, parents tend to put a great deal of stress on teaching their child to respect the rights and property of others. Sometimes they expect too much of the child too soon. A child needs time and sympathetic supervision to learn to share, to respect the rights of others, to wait his turn, and to resolve his conflicts with his peers fairly and nonviolently. Parents need to side with the child's desire to have his way, as well as preventing him from harming others and helping him see the legitimacy of other people's needs when their interests conflict with his.

We have noted already that until a child genuinely respects himself, he does not seem able to develop a genuine appreciation of the rights of others. He may make some superficial progress in learning socially acceptable behavior, and this in itself can contribute to his self-esteem. But to solidify such gains and stimulate further growth, he will need experiences that enhance his opinion of himself and his feeling that a fair proportion of the time he gets what he wants. Nature apparently decrees that our self-interest be adequately served before we can care deeply about the interest of others. This suggests that both the limits we set on our child's behavior and the methods we use to enforce those limits will affect our success in teaching him to respect the rights of others. We need to avoid pushing him too hard or too early to be "unselfish." We also had best avoid disciplinary measures that shame, or denigrate, or constantly enrage him.

Encouraging Growth Toward Independence

We have examined how concern for our children's safety circumscribes the goal of fostering independence. However, there are many ways in which parents can stimulate growth in independence within the boundaries set by the need to keep a child safe.

Becoming independent stems from having *adequate freedom to make choices*, as well as freedom to

venture out into the world on our own. It is a way
of *thinking,* no less than doing.

The more opportunities children have to choose
between reasonable and safe alternatives, the better
they become at problem solving and the more *inde-
pendently* they are able to function overall. Even very
young children can be allowed some freedom of choice
about what they will eat, wear, and do: "Would you
rather go to the store with me before lunch, or after
your nap?" . . . "have a grilled cheese sandwich or pea-
nut butter and jam?"

So, too, offering a child alternative courses of action, when he cannot be permitted to do things exactly
as he wants to, is helpful: "I can't let you ride your bike
to the movies on a weekday. Traffic is too bad. But I'm
willing to give you bus fare. Or you and your friend
could go on Sunday."

Protecting a child needs to be combined with giving him maximum independence and freedom of choice
within certain understood limits. In this way he does
not come to rely on his parents and others to do all his
thinking and choosing for him.

Of course, it is important that limits be frequently
reviewed as a child grows and becomes increasingly
competent and responsible. Increasingly, too, the child
can be involved in the family decision-making process.
He is more likely to respect limits that he has partici-
pated in setting.

Mostly, children let us know as they become ready
for increased independence. They strain at the leash.
However, since some children tend to push for more
freedom than they can handle, and others need to be

encouraged to take on more than they push for, it helps if parents know what is generally appropriate behavior in this area at various stages.

The Development of Good "Inner Controls"

From the start, parents are usually aware that a crucial goal of discipline is helping their child to take over the responsibility for regulating his own behavior, that is, to develop what are often referred to as "inner controls." Increasingly as our children grow, we cannot be present to police all their actions, nor can we have the assurance that other adults will do so. We want to be able to count on their being as careful and decent when we are not looking as when we are.

The question of what makes Johnny "behave" when we are not around is an important and complex one. Partly, children normally have a strong desire to please their parents, and so, much of the time, they make a conscious effort to do as they have been told. Partly, too, they discover early that at least some of the limits we set on their behavior make very good sense. Though a toddler may not be able to understand that streets can be dangerous, the three-year-old sees that we have a point. As a child's own experience bears out parental judgments, his parents gain considerable credit with him as being generally trustworthy guides. This shores up his respect for all their warnings and prohibitions and reinforces his conscious drive to obey them on the whole.

But still another factor, a significant developmental process, will influence the child's behavior when his parents are not around. During the preschool years he begins to identify with his parents, to make their standards of behavior his own. He acquires a conscience, which, often, "speaks" to him much as his parents would if they were present. He feels guilty about sneaking money for a popsicle from his mother's purse after his mother has said "No" to his request for it. Even if his mother does not discover his misdeed, his conscience will not let him get away with it scot-free. Similarly, his conscience will reward him—he will feel good about himself—if he resists the impulse to steal or whatever the temptation may be.

Thus the "inner controls" that we all want our children to develop will grow out of their feelings about us, their opinion of our judgment, and our own behavior. This points up a further reason for avoiding harsh physical punishment in enforcing limits. Harshness will not enhance the child's natural desire to please us, which is a big factor that we should have on our side. And through the process of identification, the child who frequently experiences harsh physical punishment may become "brutalized," may tend to deal similarly harshly with other children. The significance of parental example, of which this is one instance, will be explored further in the next chapter.

The older a child becomes, the more capacity he generally gains to "think for himself." That is, standards of behavior acquired as a result of his parents' teaching and his early identification with them are reworked in the light of his experiences in the community and his exposure to other people he admires. His "inner controls" become, indeed, his. He matures into a product of his times, and also into his own creature, though he will continue to reflect many of his parents' values.

This, too, parents should want. Too rigid a "conscience," one that does not grow with the child, is not healthy. We want our children to use their capacity for reasoning to the fullest possible extent. We can help them do this by being careful to offer honest explanations for the limits that we set on their behavior. For example, we have every right to insist that our five-year-old stop bouncing on our bed, or the sofa, but we would be wise to put our reason in terms primarily of what this does to the furniture, rather than saying, "You'll hurt yourself."

Building Healthy Attitudes Toward Authority

War-crimes trials of the seventies have given many parents pause. We do not want to rear children who always follow orders blindly. Yet there are situations in which it is important for everybody concerned that "orders" be accepted immediately, with no questions asked. We don't argue with a fireman directing traffic. Also, if we see that our child unknowingly is about to shut the door on the cat's tail, we hope that he will heed our urgent "Hold the door open" and not hear from the cat what provoked our arbitrary-sounding command.

These two considerations are not incompatible. Children can learn that sometimes it is important to "hop to" immediately and ask questions later. And they can combine this with an awareness that questioning authority appropriately is not only a right but a duty in a democracy. Both society and parents need to teach them this.

A child's parents are the first authority figures that he encounters. If they are kindly and democratic, if they will hear out his side of an argument (though not necessarily be persuaded by it), he tends to respect authority generally but question it sensibly. If his parents do not constantly order him about as if they were drill sergeants—"Come here. Get to the table. Watch your brother."—a child soon learns that an "order" signals an emergency, and he tends to respond with alacrity. In a generally democratic household, children become sensitive, too, to changes in the tone of our voice, whereas in a home where they are accustomed to being continually shouted at, they seldom recognize when an adult voice conveys special urgency.

Much that was said about parents' role in helping the child develop sound inner controls applies to building healthy attitudes toward authority. The two goals are very closely allied.

"Permissiveness"

Exercising too little control over a child is quite as bad as going to the other extreme. Children need to have adequate limits set on their behavior for several reasons besides their safety and our sanity. They may interpret their parents' failure to exercise authority appropriately as lack of love. After all, it would often be easier to let children do as they please than to take the time and energy needed to enforce reasonable limits. Children know this, really. They recognize correctly that our efforts to control them mean we love them.

Then, too, children are aware of their inexperience and vulnerability. They know that the world can be dangerous. They are also often frightened by the strength of their own emotions, their rage, jealousy, destructive impulses. In order to feel emotionally secure, they need to know that we will not let them do anything that might endanger their own safety or hurt others. If we do not offer them guidelines for moving about safely in the world, plus assurance that we will prevent them from behaving destructively until they become able to control themselves, the world will seem to them an unduly frightening place. They may run wild, hoping in this way to feel stronger, less fearful—a variation on whistling in the dark. Or, interestingly, they may become extremely timid and inhibited, showing us in this way that they are setting on themselves the limits that their elders have failed to set.

The concept of handling children permissively, giving them more freedom of choice and whenever possible reasoning with them rather than laying down the law, originally grew out of an effort to remedy some of the problems caused by the kind of parental authoritarianism that characterized child-rearing practices of the late nineteenth century. "Authoritarian" parents were widely blamed during the early decades of this century for many of the ills that beset both their children and the world, ranging from inhibitions that interfered with healthy adult sexuality to war. Certainly, the authoritarian personality is not one that most Americans would wish to perpetuate. However, some conscientious parents misinterpreted early psychoanalytical insights to mean "*Never* frustrate your child," rather than "Avoid over-frustrating your child." This led to the commission of unfortunate excesses in the name of "permissiveness," including the failure, often, to impose reasonable limits and enforce them. As a result, the word "permissiveness" currently has a very bad *cachet*, though it is only "overpermissiveness" that should be avoided.

Labels are rarely useful. They almost always lead to oversimplification. It is clear, for example, that war is the result of many complex social forces operating on the international as well as the national level, and that to view it as the product of assorted child-rearing practices simply obscures the immensity of the problem. It is time to give up making scapegoats of parents when we encounter difficulty finding solutions to the complicated social ills that beset us. So, too, parents need to give up thinking of child-rearing in terms of labels. There is no one simple solution to the job of bringing up children. A vast variety of psychological principles are involved. We need to beware of extremes of all kinds and to avoid the temptation to look for simplistic answers or "sure-fire techniques."

Punishment

For reasons already examined, harsh physical punishment, at best, makes no contribution to a child's healthy development and, if often repeated, may interfere with the socialization process. Children can be cowed, through constant physical punishment, into staying out of their parents' hair at home, but this does more to encourage them to become clever at avoiding detection than to behave acceptably. Various studies of juvenile delinquents indicate that they tend to have in common a history of frequent brutal physical punishment by parents or other caretakers.

This does not mean, of course, that brutal physical punishment *causes* juvenile delinquency, but only that it is not a way of preventing it. Parents who beat their children are usually themselves hard-pressed not just by the child, but by their life in general. Having to cope with the child, or the children, is simply the last straw. Instead of blaming them, society needs to help them and their children. A pioneering effort in this direction is described in *The Battered Child,* edited by Ray E. Helfer, M.D., and C. Henry Kempe, M.D. The book is emotionally hard to take, but citizens interested in the problem of the "battered child" may want to read it.

One more point about physical punishment: slapping a toddler's hands to set up a conditioned reflex against running into the street or engaging in other hazardous activities is not brutal. Some parents find they must resort to physical measures such as this during the early "unreasonable" years. Also, as we have seen, the majority of parents will probably occasionally hit their child in anger, even though they may strongly disapprove of physical punishment. Although this represents an admission of failure on the parent's part, a temporary giving up on trying to resolve human conflict rationally, other things being equal, it does not damage the child.

Now, what about other forms of punishment? It is imperative that a child learn gradually to accept the consequences of his behavior, which means that "punishment" in one form or another probably has to be as routine a part of growing up as it is in the adult world. If an adult accidentally breaks a neighbor's window, he will either offer to pay for it or can be brought into court and forced to do so. If a child damages the property of another, he needs to understand that restitution of some sort is expected. If he cannot afford by himself to pay for the damage, he can contribute something from his allowance, if he has one, or perform a chore for his parents who will do the paying, or for the person whose property was damaged, or he may have to forgo an expensive toy or outing that he had been looking forward to.

Although we have to make every effort to prevent our children from committing some acts of which the potential consequences are serious—running into traffic, habitually being truant from school (or perhaps, habitually failing to do homework)—we cannot and should not protect them from the discovery that all of us must pay a price for our mistakes, our errors of judgment, our forgetfulness, stubbornness, and all the rest. However, parents need to set the price their children are required to pay for any given misdeed as instructively as they are able.

Ideally, the closer a punishment reflects the way things are in the adult world, the better. For example, if a child fails to get dressed in time to leave with his brother for the movies, it could be instructive for him to miss the movie. When adults are late for a train, they miss the train. On the other hand, we do not want to be unduly harsh with our children, and, besides, we don't *always* suffer when we are late. So we might content ourselves with a warning the first time, and the second. But if we are to be good teachers, when lateness threatens to become habitual, we must make the child accept the consequences of his dawdling.

If we simply spank a child every time he misbe-haves significantly (especially if the spanking comes several hours after the deed), or deprive him of watch-ing his favorite TV program, or lock him in a closet (which qualifies as inhuman treatment if the child is afraid of the dark), we may teach him more about our power over him than about the advantages he stands to gain through governing his behavior more maturely. Still, there is no perfect approach to the problem of meting out just punishment. It is an issue that troubles society no less than parents. Circumstances will force us sometimes to actions that, in hindsight, we see as too harsh, or too lenient, or totally wide of the mark. Nonetheless, if a good proportion of the time we try to be reasonable and fair, our children will give us full points in this area. And if, mostly, through our words and the punishments we impose, we make it clear that we are not exercising power arbitrarily, but attempting to teach, our child will learn what he needs to learn.

Helping a child avoid behavior that he might later regret is always better, of course, than seeing that he accepts the consequences of his shortcomings after-ward. But it is not always possible. The best we can do is try to exact reparations for misbehavior that will help the child function more adequately in the long run, that is, truly "rehabilitate." Calling punishment by some other term, such as "deprivation of privileges," hardly makes the problem go away, though it may re-lieve some parents of their guilt feelings about it. And to say that we should never punish, but only "help chil-dren accept the consequences of their behavior," is also mincing words.

Standing Our Ground

Parents are often told to be "friendly but firm." That, too, is not always possible. Pushed enough, any of us is likely to become for the moment quite obviously unfriendly, as the word is usually defined. Being forgiving is perhaps the quality that we most need to couple with firmness. It can wipe the slate clean after tempers cool.

Should we *never* give in, once a struggle over limits is under way? Well, it is hardly advisable to reward a child's temper tantrum or similar histrionics by letting him have his way simply because he wears down our resistance. We are inviting more trouble the next time around. Also, it is quite possible that the fight the child is putting up springs from the fact that he is essentially in conflict about what he really wants to do and needs us to make the decision for him. If we give in under such conditions, he may be left feeling unprotected, frightened of his powers.

Still, every statement about rearing children has its exceptions. Parents always have to play each scene by ear. If they become convinced that they were too quick to say "No," they may decide to change course in midstream. But if this happens more than very occasionally, something is wrong either with their ability to say "Yes" or with their ability to stand their ground under fire.

Once in a while, every parent, out of weariness, or worry about more pressing matters, may say to a child, "Do whatever you please, just leave me alone." If this throwing in of the sponge is a rarity, the child will very likely be quick to sense that his victory is a Pyrrhic one;

to get his way this once is not nearly so important to him as being ensured of parental protection in the future. He may ask, "What's wrong?" or "Are you okay?" or perhaps say, "I just changed my mind. I don't think I want to do that after all." In any case, no harm is apt to come anybody's way, and parents may gain the respite they needed but couldn't bring themselves to ask for.

Being firm should not be construed as antithetical to being flexible. There are times when limits need to bend or be forgotten altogether. Landings on the moon currently take place rather infrequently, and eclipses of the moon will, in the foreseeable future, continue to be few and far between. But events far more prosaic than these may warrant a temporary moratorium on accustomed limits. Children understand, even without being told, that exceptions are only exceptions. From the fact that we make exceptions, they also can learn that it is sometimes desirable to reorder one's priorities. As one parent said, "If we aren't going to allow our ten-year-old daughter to stay up to see what happens to her favorite baseball team when the game goes into overtime, then what are we telling her to expect of life? That enjoying baseball is for boys only? That you can't have fun except at the expense of jeopardizing your health or doing your duty?"

Mothers and Discipline

There has been a strong tradition in our society of relegating to fathers, or some other male, the job of dealing with children's misbehavior. This has often been coupled with the notion that women tend by nature to be rather more easygoing and lenient with children than is really good for them. Even today one hears it said that unless children have a man to keep them under control, they tend to be undisciplined. Is there any truth in this assumption?

Available research suggests that it is not the sex of the parent but his or her approach to the challenge that matters. There have always been women who, of necessity or by choice, assumed full responsibility for helping their children learn to behave and succeeded admirably. There have always been men who preferred to leave the job to their wives. There have always been couples who shared the responsibility equally, with admirable results.

An understanding of the process of discipline is the crucial factor. Women are potentially as capable as men of setting reasonable limits and standing firm on them. The idea that men are innately better suited to the job than women probably sprang from the false assumption that discipline requires the exercise of brute force, whereas in reality what is required is good judgment—and self-confidence.

Fortunately, the policy of pushing off onto fathers the unpleasant job of meting out punishment when children misbehave is becoming a thing of the past. Most couples today recognize that this policy is neither fair to fathers nor good for children. It inevitably prevents punishment from being the kind of learning experience that it should be.

In many situations, of course, two parents together will find the going easier than one alone. When a child is being difficult, two parents who see eye to eye can give each other a great deal of needed reassurance and support. But this does not mean that a single parent, of either sex, cannot manage. One important reason that some women when left on their own are inadequate in this area is that they are convinced that no woman is up to the job. Society has made them feel that they are doomed to fail. It is a cardinal principle of psychology that a person is unlikely to be successful at any task that he or she does not feel capable of handling. The implication, then, is that in one-parent families, that parent's opinion of his or her ability to cope with the challenge of discipline is of great significance.

Accepting the Need for Continuing Confrontation

It would be ever so lovely if there were a way to bring up our children so that they would always see the reasonableness of our demands (our demands would, of course, always be reasonable, since we have read up on child-rearing) and do their growing up without forever bumping up against us.

From what is currently known about psychology, children, in order to grow into healthy adults, not only need reasonable and caring parents or parent substitutes and a reasonable and caring society, but they also need to be able, while they are growing up, to bump against sympathetic teachers, to test with impunity the validity of all that is offered to them as their "culture," that is, the sum total of what humanoids have learned in the several million years since a thumb was first opposed to a forefinger and tools started to matter.

In primitive societies parents and children did not, and do not today, live in peace. Is a certain amount of friction between the generations somehow necessary to the evolutionary process, much as the opposition of thumb and forefinger seems to be?

Nobody knows for sure. But for now, it would be irresponsible to suggest that parents, by virtue of being better informed or wiser, could eliminate such friction altogether. The struggle over limits, or, in a broader sense, the friction engendered by the socialization process, is seldom absent for long in any household, and it tends to be especially intense at certain growth stages. Since parents are older and more experienced, it is up to them to prevent the struggle from becoming a running battle of wills, or a cold war.

6

Parental Example: How It Rubs Off

OUR CHILDREN PICK up a great deal from us indirectly, by virtue of the kind of people we are, or, as a psychologist might say, by virtue of how we function in our capacity as "role models." In the preceding chapter, we touched on the way in which a child's identification with his parents, especially in the early years, contributes to this process. But throughout childhood and even into adult life, our children will, consciously and unconsciously, model their behavior in innumerable situations on the example we have set them.

The more mature our children become, intellectually and emotionally, the more likely they are to evaluate our functioning as role models critically—in the best sense of the word. That is, they recognize that their parents are not infallible, and they accept us as useful models in some ways but not others. To a parent who bridles at the idea that he might have limitations, this can be threatening. Look at it this way: if all goes well, our children can become able to profit from our strengths and let the rest go.

What Is a Role Model?

"Wow," says eleven-year-old Mark, "I really admire Mr. Moore as a teacher. You know what a drag singing assemblies used to be. Well, he's got us all taking turns using instruments like drums and triangles and rattles, and everybody actually looks forward to it, even the worst troublemakers. He has this idea that everybody has musical ability, even people like me who can't carry a tune. I sure hope when I grow up I have his trick of handling kids."

Mark's admiration for Mr. Moore suggests that the teacher's approach to "handling kids" will be an important influence in Mark's life in the years ahead. Mr. Moore is a role model who may, for example, affect Mark's functioning as a parent, not to mention his attitude toward music and possibly the arts in general.

"I'm delighted to hear that Nina gets along so beautifully with Frannie's younger brother, but it surely comes as a surprise," Nina's mother informs the mother of Frannie. "If you knew what goes on here at home between Nina and her own brother, you'd hardly describe her as a 'born peacemaker.' Though things have improved since he started school, Nina still often acts more like a child his age than a nine-year-old. Some days I think I spend most of my time just trying to help them play together happily."

Here we have a familiar story: a child whose typical behavior at home does not fully reveal the skills she

shows away from home, skills that reflect the influence of a parent as a role model. Nina's ability to play the "peacemaker" at a friend's house is an enormous tribute to the way in which her mother has handled the difficulties that inevitably arise between a brother and sister. Nina is not yet up to relating to her brother as if he were just another child. He is her brother. With other children, however, she functions as she has seen her mother function at home, exhibiting the same urge to help everybody "play together happily" and being unusually good at accomplishing it. Nina's mother's impact as a role model on her daughter's way of relating to other children is strikingly evident.

As we have seen, parents are not the only important role models in their children's lives. Teachers, relatives, family acquaintances, youth leaders, movie stars, close friends, any admired individual may, in this capacity, contribute significantly to our child's development, much as Mr. Moore is contributing to Mark's. For obvious reasons, however, parents tend to wield the most influence as role models.

What Rubs Off

Children see us whole. While Mark consciously admires Mr. Moore for "the way he handles kids" and will consciously learn from him something about that, much as one can learn about specific gravity through certain physics experiments, he may also pick up other qualities and mannerisms from his teacher. His walk, for example, or some of his gestures, or his taste in movies may, at least for a while, reflect Mr. Moore's. At one point in history, young people by the droves tended to move and talk like James Dean.

The influence of parents is also pervasive. Our children's behavior may mirror ours in innumerable ways, from how they talk on the telephone to their attitudes toward the political party in power. In areas that matter, such as political allegiance, the child will usually rethink his position in time, and, as a result, may change. He may consciously decide to modify other parental values, decide that one or both of his parents set too much store by neatness, or the social graces, and try to be less of a perfectionist in these areas.

But some very crucial attributes—such as flexibility, responsibility, regard for the rights of others, even traits such as wit, irony, a love of fun, a sense of "calling"—seem to be passed down from generation to generation, because the example of one parent or the other, or both, is irresistible—and because the child perceives what has rubbed off as a strength.

The Effectiveness of Models

As parents we spend a lot of time consciously instructing our children. We teach them how to use the telephone and the public transportation system, where babies come from, how to make change, make a bed, prepare a meal and clean up after it. We correct their manners, sometimes their homework, and over and over again their habits of dress and personal hygiene. Without in any way minimizing the value of all such teaching, it must be said that the example we set our children is at least as important, sometimes more so.

For instance, Nina's mother has probably done a lot of talking to her daughter about why the girl's actions sometimes irritate her brother, etc., etc. The mother apparently felt that the talk was largely falling on deaf ears. Yet the child, when away from the uniquely charged atmosphere that surrounds the nuclear family constellation, adopted with great skill the role she had for so long seen her mother play. So it often is with manners. A child whose etiquette at table leaves much to be desired when he is within the bosom of his family may do himself and us proud when visiting away from home, if his parents, through their behavior, have given him a clear picture of what good table manners involve.

When it comes to such matters as honesty or respect for the rights of others, parental example is especially crucial. A kindergarten teacher tells of a conference she had with the parents of a five-year-old who was unable to make friends because of his domineering behavior and quickness to hit. As she was explaining, as tactfully as she could, the difficulties the little boy was having in relating acceptably to his classmates, the father interrupted to say, "He knows better than that. We've taught him how to behave. You just have to be firm with him. At home if he doesn't do what we tell him to, he knows he'll get a licking." The teacher does not feel that she succeeded in indicating to the parents how their treatment of the boy was mirrored in his approach to other children. With her help, and the help of some of the children, he has learned to curb his tendency to bully, but she worries about what will happen to him when he comes up against the more impersonal, less sympathetic handling he is likely to encounter in first grade.

When Actions Speak Louder Than Words

"What did your teacher say when you told her you hadn't finished your social studies project?" a mother asks her fourteen-year-old son upon his return from school.

Somewhat sheepishly the boy admits having told his teacher that he had left his work at home but would bring it in, without fail, tomorrow. "It's not exactly a lie," he tells his mother as she starts to upbraid him. "I did leave my paper at home, and I will finish it tonight and get it in tomorrow. Besides, I usually hand my work in on time, and my teacher knows it."

His mother lectures him on the need to be scrupulously honest and to be willing to "pay for our mistakes," then grudgingly says that she will not report him this time, but that if she ever hears of his doing anything of the sort again, she will have to "take appropriate steps."

That evening when the boy tells his mother that Mrs. Bernard is on the phone and wants to speak to her, his mother says, "Tell her I'm not in. I know what she is calling about. She wants to know how my raffle-book sales are going, and I haven't had the time to sell any tickets yet."

Explaining Our Behavior

It happens that the mother in the preceding story recognized that there was some inconsistency between her handling of the "Mrs. Bernard incident" and her reactions earlier to her son's handling of the "social studies project incident." As soon as the boy had finished relaying her message as directed, she said to him, "I know you're busy tonight with that social studies paper, but I think I owe you an apology for some things I said, and didn't say, this afternoon. I'd like to discuss this further when you have time."

During the discussion that occurred the next day, mother and son hashed out all their feelings about "white lies" and "stretching the truth." At one point the boy said, "I know you're conscientious, Mom. You don't have to tell me." To which the mother replied, "I know you are, too. That's where I got off on the wrong track yesterday. I shouldn't have lectured you about honesty, just asked why you didn't ask your teacher for a one-day extension, considering that your work is usually done on time."

The boy allowed that he had taken the easiest way

out and wasn't exactly proud of it. "Like me with Mrs. Bernard," his mother said with a smile.

"And I'm paying now, feeling a little guilty," the boy said.

"Me too," said his mother.

As a result of the talk, the boy came away not only with the assurance that he need not hide his peccadilloes from his mother, but also with heightened awareness of the ambiguity that pervades much of life. His mother turned what might have been evaluated by the boy as an instance of parental hypocrisy into a maturing experience. By catching herself in time and presenting a role model of a different sort, she conveyed to her son a great deal through her actions and also through her words.

This is not to say that parents need to be constantly on the alert to inconsistencies in their behavior and diligent about explaining them. Children tend to take our minor inconsistencies in stride, judging us by the long-run picture. The boy meant it when he told his mother that he knew she was conscientious. Explanations are useful, on the whole, only when they open the way to needed dialogue, as in this case.

Age Makes a Difference

Very young children tend to be purists, and literal-minded to boot. Our behavior around them may need to be adjusted accordingly. Although they have to be helped to progress beyond this point, such growth usually comes slowly. The ability to accept ambiguity does not begin to be much in evidence until about nine or ten. Even a rather trivial parental white lie may be confusing to a five-year-old. He has trouble viewing such an act in proper context. So, too, parents' "kidding" of each other, even when it really is all in fun (which it often is not), can confuse a young child. He takes all our words so literally.

Many a mother, as she dishes up her three-year-old's supper, will take a bite and smack her lips in evident delight, knowing this is an excellent way to trigger the child's interest in eating and encourage him to try a "new" dish. (A few years later the child will have become sophisticated enough to see through any dissimulation in this area.) Similarly, if we want to encourage a young child to react to his grandparents and other relatives affectionately and courteously, we are careful to talk affectionately and respectfully about them in the child's presence. Disparaging comments and criticisms, however merited, are saved for times when we are alone.

Do we really need to be such goody-goodies around our children when they are little? Well, yes and no. It probably helps to extend ourselves a bit through the preschool years: watch our language; avoid white lies and other actions that a young child might misinterpret; be meticulous about observing the rules, regulations, and customs that we want our children to observe; and yes, give Aunt Maude the benefit of the doubt. If it is all that difficult for us to practice what we preach well enough to gain credibility in a small child's eyes, then perhaps we need to question some of the preaching we do.

On the other hand, even young children do not need perfect models, and they can usually detect hypocrisy. All along we have to be honest with our children, respond to all their questions with truthful answers geared to their age and maturity. Often we are required to clear up, as best we can, confusions engendered by adult behavior, including our own. Life being what it is, our children will inevitably be exposed to ambiguous, or outright undesirable, role models before we feel they are "ready." This, when handled forthrightly, need not harm the child and may be a maturing experience.

A young social worker recalls that until she was ten her father never had a steady job, and the family was on welfare. She was carefully schooled to tell anybody from the Welfare Department who might appear at their door that she did not know her father's whereabouts, although in fact he lived with the family. She does not think the experience was corrupting. She shared her parents' conviction that this one lie was, regrettably, necessary, but that otherwise lying could not be condoned. Nor did she feel that her parents were not to be trusted because they were obviously deceitful in this one respect.

Normally our children let us know when we need to let our hair down with them a bit more: "Hey, Dad, we can cross now. There's not a car in sight." Or, "How can you stand Aunt Maude? I hate going to visit her." Or, "Johnny wants me to come to his house to play on Saturday and I don't want to. How can I get out of it?" Or, "Jesus, haven't you ever heard that word before?"

Little by little over the years, our youngsters have to come to terms with us and with life "with all the warts on. " Insofar as we have any power to control that process, we play things by ear, catering as need be to the "purist" in our children in the early years and opening them up to ambiguity gradually as their behavior or experience dictates.

Sexual Identity

A great deal of serious questioning is going on these days about the extent to which differences between the sexes are culturally imposed, not simply biologically determined. Parents will naturally have their own ideas about how much differentiation between the male and the female role is desirable, but we need to be clear about the distinction between sex roles and sexual identity.

Boys and girls become aware by about age two of the anatomical differences between the sexes. If a child is valued by his parents the way he comes, he will ordinarily value his sex-determined attributes; that is, like being a boy, or a girl, along with liking himself as an individual, and look forward to functioning as a man, or as a woman. (Notice culture at work. Care to rewrite that sentence?)

However, the "if" in the above paragraph is a big one. Since boys and girls are customarily treated quite differently, both sexes get the message very early that being male or female involves far more than the anatomical differences with which we come into the world. When the doctor says, "It's a boy," or "It's a girl," the newborn is, in most cases, being assigned not only a sexual identity but also a rather rigidly defined role to play. This can complicate the child's journey toward accepting himself as a worthwhile human being who is also a member in good standing of the sex to which he biologically belongs.

Although from the moment of birth we rear our child as "a boy" or "a girl," the child does not begin to identify significantly with his or her sex for several years. Meanwhile, he, or she, is testing the temperature of the water: Is it good to be a girl? Is it good to be a boy? How are girls treated? How are boys treated? Are women nice? Are men nice?

The answers to these questions, which he obtains largely through observing his family, will affect how he comes to terms with his sex during the preschool years. From age three to five or six, the little girl ordinarily moves gradually toward identifying primarily with her mother or a mother substitute, and the little boy makes a similarly crucial identification with his father or some other male whom he admires. When this process goes well, the boy emerges proud of being male and able to appreciate women. The girl emerges equally proud of being female and equally able to appreciate men.

Both parents (or their surrogates) influence this process. In the case of a little girl, for example, her attitudes toward men are shaped not only by how her father reacts to her personally and to her mother, but also by what her mother thinks of men and how she relates to her husband. This same intricate combination of forces shapes her feelings about being a girl. Does her mother seem to enjoy being a woman and lead a satisfying life? Does her father not only make his daughter feel valued but also value women in general?

The sexes today seem in many instances to be moving toward a spirit of egalitarianism and mutual respect such as the world has seldom, if ever, seen before. It will be interesting to see how this affects the young child's coming to terms with being male or female. Will healthy adjustments be more often and more easily arrived at during the preschool years—and adolescence? Will the drama of the small child's attraction to the parent of the opposite sex be worked through with less strain on all involved? As sex roles become less rigidly defined, will the child be confused about his sexual identity, or simply relieved of unnecessary anxiety? Only time can give us the answers to such questions. All that can be said with certainty is that in order to achieve healthy sexual identity, children need to see, in the lives of the models they are exposed to, convincing evidence that one can both enjoy being a member of the sex to which one is assigned and appreciate—not exploit or fear or continually feel hostile to—the other.

Hidden Assets

The ease with which children often seem to follow parental example can be disconcerting. As one young mother of two put it: "Sometimes I think what my children do is pick up all my bad habits and none of my good ones." It does sometimes seem that way, partly because we tend to be especially sensitive to irritating traits in our children that we recognize as present in ourselves.

Hearing our daughter muttering imprecations under her breath as she bustles about getting ready for a party, we go to her and inquire, "Is there anything

I can do to help?" Back comes the answer, in almost the identical tone of voice with which we have so often responded to similar inquiries when we are bustling about the kitchen, annoyed at ourselves because something we were cooking was not going exactly as hoped for: "Yes. Leave me alone."

If we are wise, we do as requested, pondering the perversity of fate that robs our daughter, like ourselves, of the ability to be charming when frustrated by personal limitations. If we are lucky, however, we may receive from our child, as she is leaving, a hug and a kiss and a charming, "Sorry I was cross with you earlier. Forgive?" At least something good has been picked up with the bad.

Occasionally, our children's behavior may make us aware of aspects of our personality that we have previously been blind to. The annoying tendency of a five-year-old to weasel out of all his difficulties by blaming everybody and everything except himself suddenly has a familiar ring. When did we last hear something like: "It was Toby's idea to have a pillow fight and he missed the pillow so the window cracked"? Weren't we just this morning saying to that same child: "Now see what you've made me do; all your begging to have a friend over has got on my nerves so I've broken my favorite vase"? And how was it that we greeted the boy's father when he returned from work the evening before? "It was your idea to have stuffed peppers some time, so I hope you're not going to complain about dinner being late."

Although seeing how our example rubs off is sometimes painful, it may enable us to alter our own behavior as we try to help our children alter theirs. Our children are usually less interested in faulting us for our short-comings, especially if we admit them, than in relating to us as positively as we make it possible for them to do.

The Whole Picture Counts

In the course of growing up, children are not only exposed to many models other than their parents, but they also have many opportunities to "unlearn" what they have picked up earlier from the example of parents and others. Parents themselves tend to grow in the process of rearing their children. This is often reflected in changes in the kind of example they set. A rather authoritarian young father mellows, learns to listen, and actually begins to enjoy it when his children show "spirit." Family relationships take on a new tone. An anxious "mother-hen" of a young wife relaxes gradually, discovers that her children seem remarkably able to thrive without being constantly fussed over, and loses her compunction about spending time pursuing her own interests. Her children show a corresponding lessening of anxiety, and of guilt.

Changes of another kind also occur. As our children mature, they become better able to build constructively on parental example in some ways, modify a bit here, look for a different kind of role model there, make allowances overall. Inevitably, they will be different from us in a number of respects, but this need not mean that they will no longer value our love or our opinion. Mutually rewarding relations between the generations are possible at every age. We will turn our attention next to how good communication facilitates this.

7

Is Anybody Listening?

SENDING MESSAGES IS nothing. We can do it any time, without even having to fall back on words. A raised eyebrow, a slammed door, lighted candles on the dining table *say* something. But will the message be received by the person for whom it is intended? Will it be correctly understood? Responded to? Will it invite further interchange, not simply punctuate an ending?

Communication implies, to use a currently much overworked word, some kind of *dialogue*. Even dialogue need not necessarily be verbal. The infant pushes the nipple out of his mouth, and his mother puts him on her shoulder for burping. This done, she offers the nipple again, and if the child still pushes it away, or merely toys with it, she assumes that he has had enough to eat for now. That constitutes very good dialogue, or communication. A twelve-year-old leaves his muddy boots on the rug just inside the front door, and his mother, after washing them off and drying them, deposits them on his bed. The next day the boy removes his boots before he enters the house, carries them into the bathroom, cleans them, and deposits them on the toilet seat. That is both efficient and rather witty dialogue.

Words Are Important

Still, man is a verbal animal. Nonverbal communication is almost always more open to misinterpretation than communication that offers us some verbal clues to go on. A young mother who believes in the significance of "body language" admits that she can hardly wait for the day when her infant will start to talk. "I read him fine when he's all smiles," she told her own mother, "but I feel so helpless when anything goes wrong. I'm just beginning to realize how marvelous it is to be able to ask, 'Where does it hurt?' and get some kind of answer."

Conceivably, the boy in the earlier anecdote might not have noticed that his mother *cleaned* his boots before placing them on his bed—some parents of twelve-year-olds may be thinking it a miracle that a child that age should be so observant—and might have taken offense, rather than the hint. If this had happened, however, the mother could have explained her misinterpreted attempt to avoid being a nagging parent. And obviously it was only because the boy had been told many times, in words, what we do with our boots, *please*, that the nonverbal reminder worked.

As our children grow, spoken language plays an increasingly important role in our ongoing dialogue with them. Both we and they will continue, often, to respond to nonverbal cues. Parents needs to be especially on the alert for such cues when relations are strained, as happens sometimes in any family. But ironing out conflicts and problems has to be a verbal activity. Therefore, from the time that the toddler is able to speak up, we need to do all in our power to encourage his feeling that this is safe and desirable for all concerned.

Children Must Feel Respected

Respecting a child is at the core of communicating well with him. Children can be easily discouraged from telling us what they think and feel. If they discover that we cannot brook any argument or questioning of our judgment, they tend to keep their opinions to themselves, at least when they disagree with us. They may sulk, visibly, but dare not go much further. A pattern of this sort established in the early years is hard to break later on, though not impossible if parents become genuinely eager to hear what their child has to say and can tolerate dissent.

Granted, it is often trying and not infrequently impossible to reason with a preschooler. There is a point beyond which it can become ridiculous to pursue the effort. Extended conversation about why it is time now to pick up our toys, or go home, or come to supper, or go to bed seldom serves any useful purpose. After offering the obvious explanation and pointing out compensations that may help the child make the desired transition under his own steam—supper will include a favorite dessert; going to bed will bring a story—we may be reduced to picking the child up and carrying him off to where it is time for him to go.

Such incidents, even when accompanied by tears, do not violate our child's feeling that, fundamentally, we respect him. Nor will they dampen his self-assertion or his insistence on being given a reason, however unpalatable, for being required to do this, that, or the other.

Granted, too, all parents have their off days. Any "why?" somehow seems one too many, and we fall back on the time-honored "Because I say so," followed by— if it is really a bad day—"Don't talk back to me," or "You'd better get a move on if you know what's good for you." As has been emphasized so often, it is what we are usually like at our best, not what we are occasionally like at our worst, that counts.

Children *know* when they are respected. At a very young age they can already sense when we empathize with their delights, their sorrows, their fears, their unwillingness to give in to superior strength, their hurt pride, and all the other signs of humanness that even the very young of the species are heir to. It is mainly through empathizing with a child's feelings all along, letting him know through our words and other ways that he is entitled to his feelings, just as we are not only entitled but required to ride herd on his actions, that we convey respect while standing our ground. Unless we provide this kind of climate, worthwhile communication between parents and children cannot occur.

It Takes Two to Tango

All along, too, parents must take the lead in avoiding useless wrangling. Four-year-old Janie is told that she may not go to the local playground with other children in the neighborhood unless an adult is to accompany them. Her comeback is the classic one, "You never let me have any fun." If her parents rise to the bait, mutual accusations are likely to be exchanged for quite some time. Almost any parent can write the script.

But suppose that Janie's mother and father ignore the child's provocative remark. Her father responds, "I'm sorry, Janie, but we both feel it's not safe at your age, since the playground has no attendant. You'll just have to be satisfied with going when your mother or I or one of the other parents can go along."

Oh, yes, Janie will probably put up a fight for a while, but if her parents refuse to argue the point, her disappointment and anger, lacking new fuel to feed on, will subside sooner than they otherwise would. One cannot do battle for long without a real opponent.

So parents are supposed to be saints? Turn down all those stinging challenges to square off that children of every age let fly when they are frustrated? Be deaf, alike, to the young child's "I hate you" and the older one's "Wow, you sure know how to muck up things!"?

It is, of course, more than any of us can manage all of the time. We sometimes cannot resist retorting in kind, rather than simply standing firm on an issue. We want our children's love *and respect*. It is hard for us to be eternally mindful of how their position, their dependency on us for so much for so long, can cause resentment.

Benevolent and democratic though we may be, we are still more powerful than they are. They are sensitive to this difference even when we are not, and it rankles. Our ability to take their verbal flak without returning it not only helps keep the lines of communication open but also moves our children toward mature

tolerance for authority and a healthy view of how authority should be exercised.

Being Good Listeners

Not that we need submit to a tongue-lashing. The attempt to communicate rationally sometimes has to be suspended until a child calms down. A warning, such as, "Look, you're goading me," may help an older child collect himself. Younger ones may have to be temporarily isolated in a room by themselves. In some such fashion every child has to learn that our willingness to hear his side of an argument presupposes that he will exercise a certain amount of common decency in presenting it. There may be times, then, when children have to earn the right to be heard.

But family life should be made up of much more than heated confrontations. Being a good listener in general is crucial to knowing our child. What does he think of himself? Of others? Of life? He will usually tell us if we are available to listen. In the process we may be told more than we care to know about hockey standings, or the doings of some performer who has become the latest idol of the young. To dismiss his enthusiasms out of hand, however, never to try to share with him the excitement that he feels about the goal made in the last seconds of the game or the remarks made by his current television hero is to limit our chances of hearing what he has on his mind that we would very much like to know.

Why They Don't "Listen"

If a child begins to feel that communication with us is generally unpleasant, that is, consists mainly of fault-finding and admonitions, he soon tends to tune us out. Of course, every parent is occasionally perceived by his child as a nagging parent. If this is the exception rather than the rule, the child communicates his irritation to us in no uncertain terms: "Okay, okay, okay," or, "YES, Mother," or simply, "PLEASE stop nagging."

Messages of this sort suggest that it is time to take a different attitude, or a different approach, to getting those beds made, that room straightened up, or whatever else it is that we want done. Humor may help. Often it is the complaining tone of our voice, more than what we actually say, that our children object to.

That they *tell* us they object implies that communication is not in real danger of breaking down, unless that is all they ever tell us.

A certain amount of necessary reminding has to go on in every household. However, the less annoying it is to the child, the more likely it is to accomplish its aim —and not just create resistance to doing anything we might suggest.

Sometimes children literally do not hear what we are saying because they are wrapped up in what they are doing at the moment. A child may even look up dutifully from his book or cookie-making or whatever the activity may be and nod acknowledgment of our message, yet fail completely to absorb it. Reprimanding the child later for his failure to "listen" is less useful than reminding ourselves to be sure we really do have his attention the next time we have something important to say.

Of course, children have their own opinions about what is really important. They may not, for example, "listen" to us when it comes to such matters as making their bed regularly or "wearing something more appropriate," yet they may value our judgment in other areas. When they do not respond to good-humored urging on our part, it is wise for us to do some reflecting of our own. Is the matter worth making an issue of? By pressing it, might we jeopardize our child's regard for our views on more significant problems, such as the value of education, or the hazards involved in using drugs.

The extent to which our child is influenced by what we say about issues that he, too, considers important will depend, in large measure, on the overall quality of our relationship with him. Too much carping about relatively minor things can impair the quality of that relationship.

Getting Our Message Straight

If our own behavior does not jibe with the messages we send, our children may not get them straight, or, if they do, may not set much store by them. Thus, if we tell a child when we return from a trip that we missed him, yet cannot find time to sit down with him and hear what he did while we were gone, even the souvenir that we picked up for him at the last minute at the airport may not convince him that he was much missed. Insisting that our children attend religious services every week, though we ourselves rarely, or never, attend any kind of religious service, invites confusion about our values, as well as the value of religion.

Since everything that we do with our children is essentially a kind of communication, children are not, as emphasized earlier, seriously misled for long by occasional minor deviations between what we say and what our behavior appears to indicate. Our children are not going to stop respecting the property rights of others altogether just because, once, we climb over a fence clearly marked "No Trespassing" in order to picnic on the bank of a nearby stream. Nor will they lose all respect for the law upon seeing us tear up a parking ticket issued to us in a foreign country that we are about to leave. Our deeds and our words are always viewed within the context of all that they know about us.

Still, it is important that we get our message as straight as we can all along. The trespassing and the tearing up of the parking ticket should be explained to the children on the value basis that we explain them to ourselves. If we find that we cannot do this in terms that the children can understand or accept, it may mean that such incidents should not occur, at least until the children are older. Sometimes, having to put our principles into words is a sobering experience.

Mixed Messages

Parents may, without realizing it, constantly send mixed messages that seriously confuse their children. For example, a girl of eighteen, the only child of parents who are schoolteachers, severely disappointed them by refusing to go to a prestigious college to which she was admitted. Instead, she has taken a job as a sales clerk and plans soon to move into an apartment with two girls she has met at work. She explained her decision this way to a longtime friend: "After I got admitted to [name of college], all I ever heard about was the sacrifices my parents were making to give me the kind of education they always wished they'd had. I was supposed to be so lucky, and so grateful. It started me thinking. They've had my future mapped out for me since practically the day I was born, and they sure never missed a chance to tell me all they were doing without so that I could lead the life *they* wanted me to. It took me a long time to realize everything was *their* idea—the music lessons, summer camp; they even picked the colleges for me to apply to. I have no idea yet what I want to do, except there aren't going to be any more sacrifices 'for Carol's sake'."

In the fall of 1971, the small town of Harrison,

New York, was aroused by the mutilation and killing of thirteen animals in the Children's Zoo. The three high-school boys responsible for the killings were quickly apprehended. They turned out to be the sons of policemen. One father accompanied his son, sixteen, to the police station to surrender. The other two boys, brothers aged sixteen and seventeen, were brought in by detectives. Their father was quoted in *The New York Times* as describing his sons as "young and not that malicious." He went on to say: "The press should be ashamed of itself. Why don't they cover something important like the Vietnam War instead of a couple of rabbits getting killed?"

Nobody, of course, will ever know all the many factors that interacted to cause the boys to do what they did. One wonders if perhaps the atrocities of the Vietnam War, along with various sensational crimes such as the Manson murders, may have contributed by helping to bring about a social climate in which the "unthinkable" has become thinkable. Certainly, one admires the father who accompanied his son to the police station. That the other father seems to belittle the horror of the act in which his boys were involved gives the impression that these brothers may have been receiving mixed messages about where to draw the line. Obviously, far more is at work here than the possibility that a parent might have been sending mixed messages, but that possibility haunts the mind.

Getting Their Messages Straight

Children sometimes give us through their behavior important information that they cannot or do not put into words. If the parents of Carol, the eighteen-year-old mentioned earlier who has gone to work instead of to college, had been more sensitive to their daughter's behavior, they might have noticed that she always seemed a somewhat depressed child, and they might have wondered why being so "fortunate" did not make her happier on the whole.

The reading of behavior is especially necessary with little children, whose verbal facility is, after all, limited. A four-year-old, for example, cannot tell us, indeed probably does not realize, that she has been disturbed by a particular television program, but her behavior at bedtime says something is amiss. With only this clue to go on, we may make an educated guess about what upset her and eventually elicit a crucial question: "Why do Daddies hit each other, Mommy?" Aware that she calls every man a Daddy, we try to help her straighten out her reaction to an animated cartoon, and resolve not to let her watch similar programs alone for the time being.

With older children, the nonverbal messages that we pick up may be more difficult to decipher fully. The fact comes through that *something* is disturbing our daughter or son, but what? Since older children, with justification, tend to resent anything that smacks of prying, we can only be available for confidences if offered, and, perhaps, expose the child to opportunities to move in new directions. A mother reports:

Edith was really impossible the summer after she graduated from high school. We didn't know whether it had to do with boys or getting a summer job or what. We knew she followed up some leads on jobs that didn't work out. But we believed her when she said she liked the idea of being able to rest up before starting college and just do a little baby-sitting, enough to pay for a crafts course she seemed very eager to take. So we thought it was boys. But her father heard of an agency that specializes in getting jobs for teen-agers, so he told her, "I know you're probably not interested, but here's the name and here's the telephone number and here's how you get there."

The next day we had a new daughter. I could tell by the way she walked in that it was all right to ask what happened. "Well," she said, "I was scared stiff, but this woman at the agency liked me. At least, she set up some interviews for me, and I've got a job. It's not much money, and I can't take my crafts course, but I'll be a sales clerk in this great shop and help make some of the leather stuff."

The job didn't turn out to be all that perfect, but I think it was the answer for Edith right then. Any job might have been. She stuck with it. What floors me is how could she have been so scared of job-hunting after all those college interviews. I never thought of it.

Another mother has a somewhat different story to tell about getting a child's messages straight. She and her husband had decided that their fourteen-year-old son would not be permitted to go out for his school's football team, though they were willing to allow him to join the soccer team. They tried to explain to him their reasons for feeling that football was dangerous at his age, offering him several articles from medical journals to read, which he spurned. According to the mother, for two weeks during which they steadfastly refused to sign a slip permitting the boy to play football, he put up a battle such as they had never been through before. Usually rather easy to get along with, he was so nasty at home that she and her husband could not even say, "Dinner's ready," without receiving a contemptuous reply. Then the soccer season started, and things gradually returned to normal. The boy, always good at athletics, did well at soccer and seemed to enjoy it.

But the parents dreaded the approach of the next fall when once again they would be asked to sign the slip permitting their son to play football. They discussed whether, considering the way the boy was filling out as well as growing taller, they possibly should give in this time. The mother says: "If he had pushed for football, I'm afraid we would have signed." The father admits having asked his son, "You're not interested in football this year?" and receiving the reply, "Like you said, Dad, it's not worth the risks in high school." Both parents believe that their son was actually in conflict himself the first time around and had to make certain that it was his parents' doing, not his own, that kept him off the football team.

Children often battle their hardest when part of them does not want to win the fight. Parents are sometimes flabbergasted by the suddenness with which a child who has been fighting tooth and toenail to get his way may accommodate to a firm parental decision.

Often this means that the child was being pulled in opposing directions and really needed his parents, whom he perceives as more experienced than he, to make the choice for him. The messages he sends do not mean, "Give me what I am asking for," but, "Help me make up my mind."

Getting Through to Each Other

Perhaps what good communication is all about is leveling with each other absolutely, not being pressured out of thinking what we think, yet always respecting each other even when we disagree. This way, though the chips may sometimes fly, we tend to stay in touch.

Some parents apparently cannot entertain the possibility that their children might be right and that parents could be wrong. On the other hand, some parents never seem to feel entitled to their convictions. In between, there are a vast lot of us who rock along with what we feel sure of and what we are unsure of; our children cause us to change our opinions sometimes, and sometimes we change theirs. Sometimes we agree to disagree. Always, most of us live with the knowledge that we are going to be old some day and will want them really to want us. We also live with the knowledge that, for their sake, we cannot afford to back away from our convictions in the hope of currying future favors. We keep trying to communicate honestly. The overall influence that our views have on our children will depend in part on them and in part on the world we rear them in. And that we have to live with, too.

8

Tapping A Child's Potential

Parents are like mirrors constantly confronting the child with an image of what he is like and how he is doing. Naturally, the child always hopes the mirror will tell him he is the fairest one of all. If things go well for him during the early months of his life, that is pretty much the message he gets. Who can resist a smiling baby? Even the postman, the policeman at the corner, will have a try at showing off their power to evoke those delicious squeals and gurgles that make us feel we have a way with babies. Dozens of mirrors give the baby the word that he is the fairest. Then he becomes older and able to get into things and is evicted from Eden.

Of course he has to be. Each of us is only one among many, and we are no better than we are. Every child has to learn to go with that.

A Good Self-image Is Essential

However, as we help our children discover what they truly are and are capable of becoming, we need to remember that a child cannot learn to accept his limitations or discover and develop his strengths and talents unless, overall, he feels good about himself. The importance of nurturing children's self-esteem has been dealt with elsewhere, in another context, but it must be reiterated here. Those mirrors must at all times show the child that he is a worthwhile person, or he cannot make productive use of any other message they reflect.

To give just one example, a seven-year-old who is a poor sport needs to be helped to see how his behavior looks to others and how he has to modify it if he wants to get along better with his peers. His parents may find, however, that in order to help him change they must first ask themselves some questions: Why does the boy have so much difficulty with losing? What are the roots of his excessive need to "win"? Does he perhaps need help with arriving at a different definition of success? How can he be helped to feel good enough about his powers in general so that losing, when he has to, will matter less to him?

A father whose son had this problem found out that calling the boys' attention to his poor sportsmanship, no matter how tactfully it was done, accomplished nothing. He and his wife talked the situation over and decided to try a different, indirect approach. They arranged for the boy to have judo lessons at the local "Y." At first their son tended to brag rather unattractively about the new skill he was learning, but they refrained from criticizing; they concentrated, instead, on finding opportunities when they could honestly praise the boy. His mother became aware that his coordination seemed excellent for his age and commented on this whenever the occasion arose. His father found time to take him and some other youngsters bicycling regularly, which considerably improved the boy's physical prowess and his social life. Although he still has more than the usual trouble with losing, he is making some improvement in this area and is more readily accepted by other children. His touchiness has diminished enough so that his parents are now able to talk frankly with him about being a good loser.

Knowing How Children Develop

Different as every child is, children the same age have a great deal in common. They tend to be coping with similar developmental challenges, and this means that their parents have similar kinds of behavior to contend with. In other words, there is a detectable master pattern in children's growth that, to some extent, every child hews to.

Being acquainted with this pattern helps us know what to expect of our children at every stage. Of course, through observing other children in the neighborhood, parents get some impression of what children of a given age tend to be like in general. Unless our experience with a particular age group is very broad, however, we may be led astray by some of the individual differences that we come up against personally.

Our Linda, at three, can count to three. Her friend, almost the identical age, readily counts to ten and seems

to understand what the numbers mean. Is our child backward in this area? Should we work at teaching Linda to count? Actually, Linda is progressing as well as should be expected when it comes to understanding numbers. Her friend just happens to be a bit advanced.

How about Ronald, who at age four still expects his parents to dress him, although he seems bright enough compared to his four-year-old playmates? Should Ronald's parents relax and assume that the boy will begin to dress himself when he is ready? No, a four-year-old can and should do this most of the time. Ronald's parents need to look for more effective ways to encourage their son to take this step.

All along, we are required to make judgments of this sort in order to help our children progress at an optimal rate. Although children do seem to have an inborn push to grow not only physically, but in every way, it is now generally accepted that we do not just sit back and assume that a child will move ahead as he "becomes ready." Unless our expectations are appropriate—we neither expect too much nor settle for too little—healthy growth may slow down or stop altogether.

The Badge of Competence

But why does it matter, except to Ronald's parents who are stuck with dressing him, whether the boy learns to do this now or later? He seems to be progressing all right in other areas, and his playmates are unlikely to notice or care that Ronald is a bit behind in this one way.

It matters because every developmental step that

a child takes adds to his sense of "mastery," or feeling of growing competence. This is crucial to his concept of his powers. The more he is able to do, the more he feels capable of attempting and learning.

Just as children know whether or not they are respected, so they know when they are functioning as well as they should be. Although Ronald's playmates may not realize that he still has to be dressed by somebody else, Ronald himself over a number of months has been becoming aware, in various ways, that his behavior in this respect is babyish for his age. No child is pleased with such a view of himself. Ronald may already have begun to reveal, as yet too subtly for his parents to recognize, that he is not really happy about himself.

While our children may cling desperately to some particular babyish behavior, part of them always wants to be helped to give it up. Their pleasure when they finally succeed is usually very evident, and, often, they become noticeably more mature in a variety of other ways as well.

Parents are often struck by the extent to which progress in becoming toilet-trained, for example, is accompanied by more mature behavior all around. "Jeannie even looks so much older now that she's mostly dry in the daytime," says the mother of a two-year-old. Every developmental step forward of this nature tends to be marked by similarly dramatic evidence of overall growth.

Keeping Expectations Flexible

Yet, all children tend to develop somewhat unevenly. And all have their ups and downs. What a child can do today he may not be able to do tomorrow, or next week. Parents need to take in stride a certain amount of unevenness and of occasional regressing, and be not too rigid in what they expect of their child in the way of age-appropriate behavior.

But where does that leave us when it comes to getting Ronald to dress himself? We have now been informed that he should be doing this, that he knows he should, and that the longer he is permitted to lag behind, the more chance there is that his concept of himself may deteriorate. On the other hand, we also have been informed that children tend to develop somewhat unevenly, and that parents are supposed to make suitable allowances for unevenness and for ups and downs.

Beautiful. If that is not an example of putting the screws on parents, what is?

Think. The two propositions are not mutually exclusive after all. The first suggests how a knowledge of child development helps parents set reasonable goals for their child, developmentally. The second indicates how they can go about helping their child attain such goals in a reasonable fashion. If Ronald were simply very slipshod about dressing himself, one would attribute it to "unevenness." That he never tries suggests that he is somehow blocked and that different approaches to the challenge are in order.

There is some evidence indicating that children tend to respond well to challenges that their parents, or other caretakers, view as unavoidable. It appears that, often, trouble arises because parents are unsure of their ground. Their own uncertainty is communicated to the child, who interprets it as meaning that he has a choice in the situation. Once Ronald's mother is convinced that it is actually best for her child that he start dressing himself, her changed attitude may have a decisive effect. Simply saying, "Your clothes are laid out on your bed. You're big enough now to put them on yourself," and then leaving the boy to his own devices may bring the desired result fairly soon.

However, Ronald's mother should be prepared to accept occasional backsliding gracefully, responding to his "You do it today," with "All right, I'll help." Children of every age (even after they are "grown") need the reassurance that they can, if they need to, retreat temporarily into more immature behavior and a more dependent relationship with us. Allowing them these breathers from time to time enables them, overall, to push ahead.

Knowing Our Child's Own Way of Doing Things

Each child weaves his own individual variations on the master pattern of development. Parents usually begin to get a feeling for this personal pattern rather quickly. Some children, for example, seem to develop at a consistently steady pace. They master new skills gradually. Other children grow in spurts. Just when we are beginning to believe that Danny will not be ready for some time to read, or ride a bike, or take on a paper route, suddenly he romps ahead as if all the while, when he seemed to be marking time, he was really somehow preparing himself for another leap.

There are fast starters and slow starters, quick-change artists and children who prefer to take their time moving from one activity to the next. And, of course, there are marked differences in the activity level of individual youngsters; some children, from birth, can keep on the go longer than others and appear to need less sleep.

Knowing our child's special way of growing and of doing things often affords valuable clues to how he can best be helped to fulfill his potential. Teachers frequently welcome such information. A Danny, for example, presents a somewhat different kind of challenge to teachers than the youngster who progresses at a steadier pace.

Knowing What Our Child Is Coping With

On the whole, children, like adults, can give their best to a new task only when they are not faced with too many other trying demands at the same time. Thus, if a child is adjusting to his parents' getting a divorce, it would not ordinarily be desirable to transfer him to a new school if it can be avoided. Similarly, one does not start trying to toilet-train a child immediately after he has acquired a new brother or sister.

Common sense tells us this. We do not allow difficult challenges to pile up on a child if we can help it. If a youngster is having to put up with some stressful experience such as moving, or hospitalization, or illness in the family, we try to protect him as best we can from additional, avoidable stress. We also tend to be protective when we can see that the child is going through a bad time, even though we do not know what it is in himself or his environment that is giving him trouble.

The instinct to be protective under such conditions

is inherently sound. Yet there are times when a fresh challenge, which though trying in some respects might be very rewarding in others, can help a child in his struggles to handle unavoidable pressures. This is a little akin to fighting fire with fire, of course. So parents should always weigh the risks carefully and be prepared to react flexibly.

For example, four-year-old Martha was having a hard time adjusting to the birth of a baby brother. Her parents had deliberately decided against enrolling her in a nursery school, partly because of the expense but mostly because they felt it would be hard for her to adapt to being separated from her mother so soon after the arrival of the baby. However, being at home was not working out well for Martha. Her mother found it more difficult than she had foreseen to arrange to get Martha together regularly with other children, as she had done before the baby came. As September approached, Martha's parents were increasingly drawn by the idea of sending the child to nursery school, in spite of the obvious arguments against it. Finally they began calling the available schools, located an inexpensive church-connected one that would take Martha, and entered the child. "Martha had trouble letting me leave at first," her mother says, "but right from the start she loved having other children to play with. Her disposition at home was better from the day school began. I also think it was good for her to get away from the baby regularly."

Martha's parents took a calculated risk, based upon what they knew about their daughter and what she was up against. Another child in similar circumstances might not have found the opportunity to play with other children so rewarding—or have had Martha's ability to put her little brother out of her mind once he was out of her sight. It turned out that Martha was up to the challenge of nursery school and better able to work through her sibling difficulties as a result of the satisfactions gained through meeting the challenge. But whenever parents take such risks, they should stand ready to help the child retreat from the fray, if need be, without feeling any the worse for wear.

About Pushing

Life being what it is, children tend to be exposed in the ordinary course of events to situations that test them to the limit, emotionally, physically, and mentally. We do not need to create artificial challenges in an effort to' toughen our children and prepare them for getting on in the "real world." As a matter of fact, children may see any such maneuvering on our part as a subtle form of punishment or a sign that we do not really love them.

In Chapter 1, we discussed the successful father who never gave his sons allowances in keeping with his means, hoping in this way to teach his boys the "value of money." We saw how his efforts misfired. The boys felt abused and viewed their father as stingy and unloving.

Along the same lines, a father who was worried because his son seemed physically "soft" decided to send the boy, at age sixteen, to a summer camp that afforded "experiences in surviving in the wilderness." The boy did not want to go, but the father insisted, asserting that if he were later drafted into the armed forces he would be grateful to his parents for having seen to it that he got himself into shape. After three days at the camp, the boy ran away. His parents, with some psychological help, eventually accepted the fact that the boy was not going to go along with any such efforts to toughen him up. At twenty-one, after graduating from college, this young man joined the Peace Corps and went to a remote village in Africa. His parents were sure that he would fall ill or tire of the life in short order, but he loved his assignment and adapted to primitive living conditions with no difficulty.

Nevertheless, our children do need us to help them properly evaluate and face up to the very real challenges that life presents them with. In the process, if we use our influence wisely, we can move them toward maximum development of their potential.

Why not just come right out and say that sometimes we ought to push our children? The point is that "pushing," to be effective, must come from within the child. We can do our best to help him see the desirability of trying this, that, or the other. But our efforts will come to very little unless the child decides to push himself.

Parents can, for example, expose their child to many different kinds of intellectually stimulating experiences that encourage a youngster to develop his mental abilities to the fullest possible extent. They can take him to museums and other cultural centers, see that he has a library card and a quiet place to study, be available to help with homework when requested, show interest in his school work, and talk with him about the issues of the day, books, television programs that the family watches together, and any other subjects that arouse his curiosity. However, in the final analysis, we cannot make our child exert himself intellectually. Only he can do that.

Evaluating Real Challenges

Children do not always want what they need, or even know what they want. Here is where parents can be extremely influential and helpful.

We mentioned a boy who resisted his parents' efforts to "get him into condition." Those efforts, while well meant, were obviously misplaced. Yet, one suspects that the parents missed some good opportunities to help the boy enjoy physical activity while he was growing up. Obviously, he had the potential for this, as most children do. Unfortunately, in our sports-oriented society, many children at an early age acquire a poor image of themselves physically and react by "not liking" many of the competitive sports that are popular with their peers. They tend to be wary of joining in any activity in which their performance is apt to be compared with that of the other participants. When they say, "I don't like baseball," or bowling, or basketball, what they often mean is, "I don't like my inability to play it as well as most of my friends."

Parents cannot overcome the culture single-handedly (though occasional small victories in terms of a school's physical education program may be possible). However, we can do a number of things to help our children view themselves as something other than bumblers and enjoy the uniquely satisfying experience of exerting their physical powers to the limit. Sports such as swimming and skating are less likely to invite unkind comparisons. If we help our child acquire minimal skill at them, he usually will enjoy them. Bicycling, hiking, and modern dance classes appeal to many. Often a child who is set against organized camping enjoys going camping with a parent, or the family, or good friends.

Children's resistance to testing their powers in any area—social, physical, mental—generally means that they have not come up against the right challenges under the right circumstances. Not that a child has to be well rounded in the popular sense of the phrase. Aiming specifically for that may hinder a youngster from finding out who he really is, and enjoying and developing that self. We must always respect our child's individuality when working to prevent him from locking himself into imaginary limitations.

Parents are often called upon, too, to help a child sort out conflicting challenges. Laurie has been invited to participate in an experimental foreign-language program in her school, but it would mean that she would be separated from her friends in all her classes, and Laurie does not make friends easily. Since she is only fifteen, her parents can play a crucial role in alerting her to all the pluses and minuses that might be associated with each choice, and in helping her live with the decision that she finally makes.

Real Weaknesses

Donald is very nearsighted and somewhat clumsy. Even with his thick-lensed glasses, he does not always see well enough to move about confidently and quickly. He hates organized athletics. The year he was ten he pestered his parents to ask his eye doctor for a slip excusing him from physical education. After discussing the matter, Donald's parents refused. They talked with him about possible ways of dealing with the teasing that his athletic shortcomings sometimes exposed him to, and suggested that, since nobody is good at everything, perhaps this was the time to come to terms with feeling inadequate.

Donald was not happy with that decision, but in time he stopped complaining about it. He has not since raised the question of getting excused from physical education. At fourteen, he has become, in his words, "the world's greatest loser—I had no choice." Recently, during a school field day, Donald's performance in the potato race gave rise to a few titters. As he crossed the finish line last in his heat, he shrugged his shoulders and said, "Well, you can't win them all." This brought a burst of appreciative laughter, and Donald walked off, as usual, with several friends slapping him on the back and cheering him.

Donald has learned to compensate well for his athletic limitations, without closing the door on the eventual possibility of lessening them to some degree. Last summer he had a job caddying on the local golf course, took a few lessons, and found he has a genuine knack for the game.

In helping our children accept and compensate for their weaknesses, it is important that we not rule out all hope of any improvement. True, there are disabilities, physical and mental, with which a child is born and

Dear madame Jan. 1973
Please excuse
my son from physical
training

166

with which he must learn to live as best he can throughout his life. Such disabilities must be viewed realistically by parent and child alike. Yet, nobody can foretell for sure the extent to which they might be compensated for in this way or that.

We do not want to push our children constantly into situations that will inevitably bring disappointment and defeat. Nor do we want them constantly to push themselves into such situations. On the other hand, we need to fish with a long line. We cannot afford to set a rigid ceiling on a child's potential in any direction; what he could not do yesterday, he just may be able to do tomorrow.

Parents and teachers need always to be ready to revise their estimation of a given child's capacity, and ready to offer him the opportunity to stretch himself. Shy, quiet Ruth, whom nobody ever thought of as having leadership ability, volunteers to chair an assembly meeting on racial issues that have been troubling her high school, gets the job because two other students give up trying to handle the meeting, and manages to bring some kind of order out of chaos. The teacher who had beckoned Ruth to the platform said later, "Sure I was as surprised as anybody else when Ruth volunteered, but I have a lot of respect for her, and I figured if she thinks she can do this, let's see."

Talents

Most people seem to think of talent as inborn, and that is at least partially correct. However, although there may be limits to what we can draw out of a child, it is clear that all children are, in their way, "creative."

On the whole, we seem to know more about what puts a damper on that creativity than about how to encourage its flowering—in writing, music, art, science, or areas such as politics or business administration.

Is talent, then, synonymous with creativity? Both words stand for qualities that are hard to describe but immediately recognized when encountered. (The Austrian philosopher Ludwig Wittgenstein, in discussing the meaning of the word game, has called attention to this oddity in the functioning of language.) It may be that creativity is what makes "talent"—defined for the time being as a special aptitude of mind or body—matter. Perfect pitch, manual dexterity, and determined practice produce many a pianist capable of earning a good living as an accompanist. Without all three qualities, only two of which are inborn, Johnny is unlikely to get far as a pianist, although all through his childhood people observing the inborn qualities may say, "That boy has talent." Going a step further, Johnny may make it as an accompanist but fail to get beyond that point. He has the technical proficiency, but not that something extra that distinguishes an accomplished accompanist from the musician whose name goes down among the greats. And that something extra? It isn't the "ear," or the dexterity, or the hard work, but—for want of a better word—creativity.

So we do not try to make a musician out of a tone-deaf child—though we do operate on the thesis that music can be a lasting source of pleasure to any child who is appropriately introduced to it. And we do our best not to kill the creative effervescence, the free play of the imagination, that all children appear to bring into the world, though perhaps in varying amounts.

Some psychoanalysts, such as Dr. Lawrence Kubie, suggest that the educational process, meaning not only the educational *system* but acculturation in general, is inherently at odds with the child's creativity; some loss of spontaneity and imaginativeness may be the price we have to pay for becoming civilized. At the same time Dr. Kubie questions some standard educational practices, notably the idea that all children need to attend school throughout the school "day" and the school "year," and the deadly dullness of much drill, which, though it may be essential to learning, could be made more stimulating.

Many educators today are concerned with the stultifying effects of our lock-step system, which in the Western world, at least, has for several centuries been something of a sacred cow. Needed innovation may finally be in the offing.

Meanwhile, what can parents do to protect their children's natural creativity while helping them discover and develop their talents? Again, it seems to be a matter of leading the horse to water but accepting the fact that we cannot make him drink. Overloading a youngster with organized after-school lessons and other activities may deprive him of time needed to explore his world imaginatively and innovatively, as well as being hard on his health. Pushing a child, in music, art, or anything else, is not truly productive unless the child's interest is fired and he begins to move ahead under his own steam. Mozart's father, who is sometimes cited as an example to the contrary, did not begin to bear down on his son until the boy had exhibited both

intense interest and extraordinary talent.

One can speculate for hours about how much talent goes undeveloped. That persons cast in the role of rejects by our schools and society occasionally manage, under the unlikeliest conditions, to educate themselves and exhibit remarkable brilliance—as in the case of Malcolm X or Eric Hoffer—should give us pause.

Society must work with families in tapping the potential of all children. Only in this way can we be assured that every child will be exposed to the variety of experiences necessary to enable him to discover his interests, strengths, and talents, and that he will have access to the facilities and adult guidance needed to cultivate them to the fullest extent. The indomitable geniuses among us may perhaps manage to surface regardless of the obstacles placed in their way. Even so, the scarring that sometimes occurs is appalling. That the obstacles are insuperable for some children seems clear and is a tragic loss for them and for society.

Nothing Succeeds Like Success

Having started with the assertion that a child must have a good opinion of himself, or a positive self-image, before he is able to accept and learn from criticism, we have now come full circle. The cliché that nothing succeeds like success contains profound psychological truth.

In any society, however, it inevitably raises the question of values. How do we define success? Though Americans are accused of being materialistic, few if any of us would define success totally in terms of the marketplace. Nor do we bring up our children to do so. This may account for some of the outrage that is evident among youth today. The discontented young have taken to heart what we told them was essential to the good life, and they cannot reconcile this with what they see in society and, sometimes, in their parents' own lifestyle. They want the world to conform more nearly to ideals that we ourselves instilled in them. Their impatience, though typical of the young, is also rather typically American. Both their nonviolence and their violence have been come by legitimately. In a country that was founded by, among others, Quakers and refugees from debtors' prison, that came into being by way of a revolution, that has bred slave traders and abolitionists, espoused slavery and outlawed it, many traditions and values, often conflicting, are as American as apple pie.

Within this welter of values every parent has to pick his way and come to terms with what constitutes success. Our children initially need to see themselves as successful in our eyes in order to keep growing. In the early years, especially, it is mainly we who confer the badge of competence on them, searching out, if we must, activities for them to succeed at.

What we value or do not value comes through covertly, as well as directly. If, for example, we secretly admire a child's ability to make his way with his fists in the world of his peers, he may, despite all our admonitions against fighting, see this as the road to success unless other role models convince him differently. If we value winning at any cost, competitiveness may become a crucial pressure in his life, though he may depart from our opinion of who the winners ought to be, or may even decide that it is evil to compete.

Still, in spite of the ambiguity involved in helping a child become what he is able to become, some principles emerge: we must help him feel good about his powers; we must help him see and accept the consequences of his behavior, serving as both mirrors and interpreters; we must give him all the opening-up experiences that it is within our power to expose him to; we must urge him on—but mindful of the hazards involved in excessive pushing—when, because he is young, he is sometimes too easily sidetracked; we must remember that society and the child himself share with us the responsibility for the ultimate outcome.

9

The Beautiful Times

HALLOWEEN? THE PARENTS of the girl who wrote the following letter were startled to learn that Halloween was a holiday that meant something to a seventeen-year-old.

Dear Mother, Daddy, Lee, Win, Circus, Turtle and fish:

Today for the first time since I've been here I am a little homesick. I woke up thinking about the house being all decorated, so after my morning classes I went down to Thayer St. and bought a pumpkin—very small, the big ones are so expensive!—but it looks cheery on my desk. This afternoon Rachel and I went out with two shopping bags and gathered oak leaves and spread them all over our floor! Our neighbors must think we're

172

kooks, but our room smells delicious. Anyway, happy Halloween . . .

—from a letter from a college freshman

Had they made that much of it over the years? A few cardboard skeletons that were practically as old as the girl herself, some rubber spiders hanging from ceiling light fixtures and in doorways—was that decorating? Of course there was always the pumpkin and the traditions surrounding it. The pumpkin had to be the biggest they could find. For a while, it had to be too heavy for the baby in the family to lift, but the youngest was now five, and that tradition had long since been outgrown. As for going trick-or-treating, the writer of the letter had given that up some years before she went away to college. *Halloween* mattered?

Much Eludes Explanation

All along we have emphasized the complexity of human nature and the multiplicity of factors that affect a person's reactions in any given situation. Nowhere is this more evident than in the capacity to feel joy.

In the foregoing letter, many currents of emotion can be identified: nostalgia; fondness for family, home, traditions, and holidays; a high opinion of spontaneity, individualism, having fun, being a self-starter. Yet who is to say that if we manage to rear children who value and exemplify these traits, we guarantee them their share of beautiful times?

And who knows all that was going on in the girl who wrote the letter? Obviously, memories of Halloween were not the only or even the major influence at work. They merely triggered feelings about home and about holidays in general, along with nobody knows how much else.

Then why try to discuss children's capacity to be joyous if it is so difficult to dissect? The reason is that it is widely recognized as a key factor in mental health. A characteristic of such significance deserves to be examined as best we can.

Is It Inborn?

In discussing creativity in the previous chapter, we suggested that all children are born with the capacity to be creative, though possibly they possess it in varying degrees. This also appears to be true of the capacity to enjoy life. Only sick or severely deprived babies are characteristically listless. In fact, listlessness in a baby who is receiving adequate mothering is often a sign of the onset of illness.

We have all witnessed the delight with which small children so often respond to the world around them. We know how easily they move from tears to laughter —as well as *vice versa*. The troubles of a healthy pre-schooler, intense as they may be while they last, are typically shrugged off as if by magic when pleasure beckons.

Is this because young children have short memories? Or because their native capacity to enjoy whatever is around to enjoy has not been diminished by guilt and other burdens that adults frequently bear? We do not really know. It could be a mixture of both factors.

We do know, however, that joyousness can be all but extinguished in a child at a very early age. This is not something that can happen only later in childhood, or in adult life. Some decades back, Dr. John Bowlby and others called attention to the fact that children in institutions, whose physical needs were well met but who received no cuddling or other kinds of affectionate attention, were generally listless, failed to thrive, and often died—simply from lack of love. Institutions are now generally aware of this problem and make an effort to provide their charges with what they refer to as TLC, meaning tender loving care. Even so, more recent studies of young children in certain institutions in this country indicate that despite some improvement—apparently institutionalized babies are no longer dying from lack of affection—many such babies are remarkably joyless. They seldom smile and are noticeably slow to respond to an invitation to play. (Their intellectual development is also markedly slowed.)

Although this does not tell us how to nurture joyousness, it does alert us to some conditions under which it will almost surely be destroyed and documents the seriousness of its absence. Children without families, or with families so beset by problems that the child is deprived of adequate adult attention and affection, early lose an important ingredient of emotional health. There is some evidence that the process can be reversed, but only as the result of years of good "mothering" by a parent or parent substitute.

The "Happy" Child

From the beginning, hurt and frustration are a part of every child's life. There is a limit not only to our power to protect our children but also to the desirability of protecting them from everyday frustrations. Children have to learn to accept the consequences of their behavior, to respect the rights and needs of others, and to shoulder appropriate responsibilities. This is not always easy, to put it mildly.

Just as every child, however emotionally healthy he may be, experiences problems in the course of growing up, so he lives through a great deal of unhappiness. Yet if he can enjoy himself when the conditions are right for that, we correctly identify him as a "happy" child.

As children grow, they become more adept at concealing their true feelings from us. However, parents can usually tell when a child is basically happy and when he is continually joyless. During adolescence, moodiness is especially common. Yet, if in spite of this the child retains the ability to react with obvious, wholehearted pleasure to some aspects of his life, there is good reason to believe that he is coping adequately with his problems. Prolonged absence of any genuine joyfulness is grounds for concern, even if the child shows no other serious problem behavior. A depressed child may be as much, or more, in need of psychological help as a destructively rebellious one.

Spontaneous Delight

Some of the joy that we experience comes as a reward for effort and planning. The college girl whose letter was quoted earlier deliberately set out to cheer herself up. However, the beautiful times often come unexpectedly. Frequently, like sunsets and rainbows, they are beyond our willing. So, too, is our openness to them.

The spontaneous delight that small children are capable of touches a responsive chord in many of us. We enjoy the child's joy. For a moment the child may even enable us to see and feel freshly again some of the wonders around us that we long ago ceased to give thought to. Yes, the spider's web with dew on it is like fairyland. The steam shovel does huff like a great big bulldog. Night, when all the lights come on, is the most exciting time of day in the city.

When we can share our children's delight, both we and they gain. If we heed that request, "Come and see," we may return with renewed energy to our necessary duties. Our action enhances our child's special pleasure and also says to him that joy is an indispensable part of living.

Sometimes we may be the ones who are riveted by a sense of magic that escapes our child. "What's so great about walking under cherry trees? I want to climb the monument." "Please, can we stop talking history now and go swimming?"

We have the same right to our enthusiasms and excitements as our children have to theirs. If mutual sharing is not possible, mutual respect always is.

Of course, a child's age will affect his interests and attention span. There is a limit to how long a small child should be expected to bear with us while we enjoy the cherry blossoms. Still, even with small children, there is room for a certain amount of give and take in this area.

It is good for children to see us stop and linger with rapt absorption over discoveries that fascinate us. In this way, as role models, we reassure them that each

of us is entitled to our own fun. Though our particular
interests may not rub off on our children, our attitude
toward life does.

Celebrations

Holidays and other occasions that are made much
of in a family year after year have an enormous impact
on children. Such family traditions probably matter a
great deal more to everybody concerned than is realized
at the time. The child's anticipation of the great event
is evident all right—for days in advance. Sometimes it is
so evident that adults are tempted to take advantage
of the situation: "You'd better be a good girl or Santa
won't come to see you."

It is easy to be a purist about such blatant attempts
at bribery. Ideally they should not occur. Yet parents,
tired and envious—yes, envious of the child's carefree
excitement—sometimes yield to temptation. Eventually,
of course, the child will realize the extent to which he
was tricked through that particular device. But if he
feels that the reward was always there, regardless, he will
probably decide that his parents deserved whatever
respite they gained through their ploy. Once more, it is
the whole picture that counts.

The truly beautiful times that a family enjoys together tend to be relived over and over. In recollection,
they often take on an added glow, a heightened power
to bind us together. Minor disasters—the pumpkin pie
that caught fire in the broiler and burned to a crisp,
the homemade chicken paté that became the dog's
Thanksgiving dinner before the family had a chance to
sample it—such episodes achieve the status of conver-

sation pieces in time. Their annual retelling adds to the shared warmth and festive spirit of the occasion.

As we all know, children often measure time in terms of holidays and other celebrations that they have learned to look forward to. The passing of the year is marked for them not so much by months, or seasons, as by birthdays and occasions such as Hanukkah or Christmas, New Year's Day, Valentine's Day, St. Patrick's Day, April Fool, Passover, Easter, Fourth of July, Rosh Hashanah, Yom Kippur, Halloween, Thanksgiving. One holiday is scarcely over before they are counting the days to the next.

And why not? Holidays are meant to be a time of joy for everybody involved. Though some of them are in part solemn occasions, even these are intended to include festivities and rituals that lift the spirits. Such celebrations have an honorable tradition going back to the dawn of civilization. They are particularly emphasized in primitive societies and among oppressed groups whose lives are conspicuously lacking in other pleasures and satisfactions, for example, first-generation Americans of various ethnic origins. Quite possibly, as some social psychologists have suggested, ritualized feasting is a saving source of emotional health for people who would otherwise have scant opportunity to experience joy.

One of the sad things that has happened to the affluent in our society is that, in some cases, they no longer really enjoy many of our traditional holidays. The commercialization of some, such as Christmas, has turned an entire holiday season into such a hectic, demanding period for adults that, often, the rewards hardly seem to justify the effort. For days on end, parents are too tense and tired to be happy. Children know when this happens, and a damper is cast on their native ability to be joyful.

Joy and Sorrow

We are all aware that joy and sorrow are not really opposing emotions, that, in fact, like tears and laughter they are often intermingled. As we sit listening to a favorite piece of music, reveling in the perfection with which it is being played, we suddenly find ourselves with a lump in our throat. Or, in the midst of a lovely day at the beach, the glow of happiness that we have been feeling is momentarily shot through with an inexplicable tinge of sadness, which somehow adds to our appreciation of the occasion. Could it be that the *most* beautiful times are those that evoke a spectrum of emotions?

Young children tend to be purists in this as in other areas. "Why are you crying?" the five-year-old demands when he sees tears spring to our eyes at the sight of the birthday present he has made for us. It will be some years before he will find out for himself, perhaps at a surprise party or upon receiving an unexpected compliment, that human beings often cry, or feel like crying, when they are very happy.

Yet every toddler and preschooler who is capable of being joyous is also easily moved to tears and anger. Their reactions in any given situation may be more simplistic than ours, but they are obviously capable of a broad range of emotions. Interestingly, marked joylessness is generally associated with what is technically termed "emotional flatness," that is, a blunting of the entire repertoire of normal human feelings. Such children (and adults) not only show less joy, but also less anger and all the other emotions.

Implications for Parents

This fact lends support to the assumption that the ability to enjoy life has complex roots. Certainly we should do what we can to provide our children with opportunities to enjoy themselves. We also need to put our seal of approval on pleasure by sharing their joys to the extent possible. However, still more seems to be called for.

What little we know indicates that it is important for us to make our children understand that they are entitled to *all* their emotions. Of course they have to learn to control their behavior. However, in the process of helping them accomplish this, we must be very careful not to imply that we blame them for how they feel. We need to assure Amy that we understand her feeling angry at her little brother. She has every right to be mad when he grabs one of her crayons and scribbles on her drawing. It is her *actions* that require controlling. We will not allow her to hit her brother on the head with her coloring book.

In our capacity as interpreters of how our children are doing and what they are up against, we want to be sure that we do not rob them of any of their spontaneous emotional reactions to life. Our job is to help them accept all their emotions, not feel guilty about them, while at the same time insisting that they handle their feelings in a socially acceptable fashion.

But what if we really do not think our child is entitled to feel as he obviously does? Then we express our puzzlement honestly, but in a way that does not pooh-pooh the child's emotion, or condemn it, or attempt to analyze it: "I see you're very angry with your teacher, Michael. What I don't see is why. The way you tell it, he had to send you and your friend out of the classroom in order to get the attention of the others. I'm sure you were being very funny, but he has his job to do. He must like the two of you, or you would have found yourselves in worse trouble." This sometimes invites our child to turn his anger on us, and he may do so initially. Through being accepting as well as honest, however, we give him the opportunity to think over his emotions without feeling threatened by them. As a result he may revise his opinion of his teacher.

Sometimes children may need us to help them admit what they are feeling. No matter how accepting we may be of tears, anger, fear, etc., our child may still find it difficult to acknowledge them. After all, parents are not a child's whole world. In some circles, as even a three-year-old usually knows, boys are not supposed to cry or show fear, and no child is supposed to feel angry at adults. In addition, some children may find it harder than others to face up to their real feelings. Perhaps they feel more intensely, which makes emotion potentially more frightening to them; or perhaps they have a stronger desire to please, or to be like, adults, and this seems to them to demand repression of strong feelings. Or unknown factors may be at work. At any rate, they become emotionally guarded and need us to help them keep in touch with their feelings.

A simple statement such as, "It must be hard on you when people make such a fuss over the baby. You're very nice about it," both compliments a child on his self-control and helps him acknowledge to himself that he feels resentment—and has a right to do so. In such ways we can give a child leave to feel angry or hurt or disappointed or whatever, while at the same time patting him on the back for behaving well.

One word of caution: parents are not supposed to be therapists. We do not say to a child, "Doesn't that make you fighting mad?" Such a question might undermine all his hard-won inner controls. We must always ally ourselves firmly with the child's control, or "better nature," when notifying him that he is entitled to whatever emotions may be churning around inside him. To reiterate, we never try to analyze those emotions, or argue with a child about what he is feeling.

A therapist should be consulted if we think our child is seriously overcontrolled. All we are supposed to do is acknowledge the possible existence of hard-to-handle feelings at the same time that we encourage socially acceptable behavior.

Facing Up to Our Own Feelings

Again, some of the more important teaching that we do is through example. Parents' ways of handling their own emotions tend to rub off on their children. As indicated in earlier chapters, this can be disconcerting from time to time, as we watch our children mirroring aspects of ourselves that we do not admire. We need to keep reminding ourselves that over the long haul our youngsters will be exposed to many role models, and that there will be many opportunities for us and others to help them modify their behavior. The way young Sara now mimics the least attractive of our methods of dealing with our anger is open to change.

Children test parental self-control in innumerable ways. All of us lose our tempers from time to time, which, as already indicated, need not do any harm and may under some circumstances be salutary. Letting a child know when he is annoying us is definitely salutary. It may have a calming effect all around. There are times, though, when parents do not realize that they are annoyed with, or resentful of, their children because they have no "acceptable" reason to be so.

How dare we resent our children just because rearing children is a very expensive, time-consuming business? How can we possibly blame them for the fact that but for them we might be enjoying a carefree existence, going out nights when we felt like it, taking some of those fabulous trips advertised in the newspapers and on TV, quite possibly owning our own home by now, etc., etc. No, it is unthinkable that parents should entertain such selfish feelings, and obviously *we* do not. We love our children, have never for a minute regretted having them. If they do not always seem to appreciate everything that we have done for them, well, that's the nature of children.

It is true that we love our children and are glad we have them. Occasionally, however, our love may be mixed with resentment or disappointment—through no fault of the children. If we can accept the truth that we, too, are entitled to our feelings, we are less likely to punish our children and ourselves unconsciously for our "unreasonable" resentments by playing the martyr or making life difficult for everybody in other ways.

Unadmitted resentment and disappointment have a way of leaking out around the edges of our self-control. The child feels that something is wrong, though he cannot put his finger on the trouble or how he may have contributed to it. He feels somehow at fault and does not know what to do about it.

Facing up to our difficult feelings is not guaranteed to make them go away immediately, but it does enable us to handle them more rationally. We catch ourselves being unusually demanding or picky or short with our child and say, "Look, I'm in a bad mood. It's not your fault. I'm sorry." The child senses that all three statements are true, and no harm is done. If, as often happens, he also concludes sensibly that this is a day to stay out of Mother's (or Daddy's) hair, we will probably be the better for it, and he none the worse. Children can cope with our off days if such days are not too frequent and if it is clearly understood by us and by them that they are doing us a special favor. In fact, such experiences can be maturing.

Fun and Responsibility

Just as the beautiful times have to be considered within the context of the entire range of human emotions, so fun is linked to responsibility—and not just in the minds of puritans. The two need not be antithetical. Ideally they reinforce each other.

When our children are very young we start teaching them that their freedom to have fun has certain well-defined limits designed to ensure their safety and that of others: no playing with sharp objects, no throwing sand. Gradually we go further and teach them to respect less obvious rights and feelings of others. We help them learn to have fun *responsibly*. If we are careful not to interfere with a child's fun capriciously, he accepts the value of such limits, even though he may not always abide by them. In time he also learns that he has responsibilities of various kinds—toward his school work, toward the functioning of the household —that take precedence over having fun.

As we help our child move slowly from playing responsibly to being a responsible person in every respect, we need to be sure that we do not, intentionally or unintentionally, rob fun of the status it deserves in our lives, turn it into a sort of second-class citizen. Joy, as surely as bread, is the staff of life. We must have both.

10

Having the Children You Want—and No More

PUBLIC OPINION POLLS conducted in recent years show that the vast majority of men and women in this country are in favor of birth control. We shall discuss some reasons for limiting family size and controlling the spacing of children; methods of birth control, including experimental approaches that may become available in the future; advances in treating infertility; and adoption as a means of having children when one is unable to conceive, or of enlarging one's family without contributing to the population explosion.

Family Planning as a Social Responsibility

Many scientists today are convinced that if voluntary family planning efforts do not bring about, within a very few years, a stable world population, governments will have to step in and limit, through some form of licensing, the right to give birth. This is not a pleasant prospect, but neither is the prospect of living with runaway population growth, as indicated in Chapter 2. Family planning, then, needs to be viewed as a social responsibility, as well as a matter of simply personal privilege.

Nowadays, numerous ecologists and others concerned about world population problems are recommending that couples have no more than two children of their own. Even this would result in a population increase in the United States for another decade or two. At present our population is composed of an unprecedentedly large percentage of young people entering upon childbearing years. The generation born during the so-called baby boom that followed World War II is now having its own babies.

Medical Considerations

There are many sound medical reasons for a woman to limit the number of children she bears and to control the timing of her pregnancies. Statistics indicate that, safe as childbearing has become, the risks it involves for both mother and child tend to increase with repeated pregnancies. They are several times higher for the woman having her fifth baby than for the woman having her second. After two or three deliveries, the uterine muscles gradually lose their tone and function less forcefully and effectively during the birth process. Other problems, such as varicose veins, anemia, hemorrhoids, and back troubles, also tend to be more common. Mortality rates rise for mother and child, and the incidence of birth defects is higher.

The spacing of children and a mother's age when

she gives birth also make a difference. Obstetricians generally agree that the optimal spacing of children is approximately two years apart. This allows the mother's body time to recover fully from pregnancy and giving birth, yet her muscles still retain some of that extra capacity for stretching that a previous delivery gives them. As you would probably expect, statistics indicate that the incidence of problems of various kinds is significantly higher for mothers over age thirty-five. What you might not know is that this also holds true for mothers in their early teens. Mortality rates, for both a mother and her infant, are at their lowest when a mother is between the ages of twenty and thirty-five. Birth defects and complications during pregnancy and delivery are also lowest during this age span.

It would be a poor world, certainly, if we allowed ourselves to be governed entirely by statistics. They never take into account all the factors that enter into a given situation. For example, if you don't marry until your late thirties—or remarry then—there is no reason to fear having a baby as long as you are healthy and have good medical care. However, women (and the men who care about them) deserve to know the statistics relevant to making childbirth as safe and easy as possible, so that they can exercise as much freedom of choice as is available to them and evaluate their various options wisely.

Other Considerations

Many young couples desire to limit the size of their families for financial reasons. Children today are a luxury, especially if parents wish to provide their youngsters with "extras," such as summer camp, lessons in music or dance, a college education, and all the other experiences and equipment and medical care that can enable a child to develop his potential in all directions to the fullest possible extent. A young father was recently startled to discover that, in his words, "It's going to cost us as much to get our daughter's teeth straightened as it cost my parents to see me through braces and college both."

Another factor that may make parents want to limit the number of children they have is the growing awareness of the degree to which a child's, intellectual development is affected by the amount and kind of adult attention and stimulation that he receives during the early years, starting right after he is born. We now know that "good mothering," by a parent or parent substitute, not only enables a baby to thrive physically and emotionally, but also plays a critical role in cognitive, or mental, growth. Babies and young children need the stimulation of being played with, talked to, reacted to, introduced appropriately to new experiences, and offered a change of scene from time to time in order to insure maximum development of their mental capacities. When there are many children close together in age, it is more difficult for parents to ensure that each has the individual attention and constructive stimulation from an adult that is so important during the early years.

Then, too, an increasing number of young women are deciding that although they want the experience of being a mother, and possibly the experience of being a full-time mother for several years, they will want to pursue a career for most of their adult life. They are ready to drop out of the labor market long enough to get one or two children "off to a good start," but that is all the children they are interested in having.

Aren't Large Families Good for the Children?

There is no "ideal" family size. Though one often hears ominous warnings about the fate of only children, no available research indicates that, statistically speaking, they are any less likely to grow up emotionally healthy and be successful in life than children from larger families. A hundred years ago, when our society was still predominantly an agrarian one, an only child was quite often a lonely child. This may, in part, explain why some parents today still feel that they owe it to their offspring to provide him with a brother or sister, or several of both. But in our world today, playmates are generally easy to come by and provide the only child with the companionship and experience in relating to other youngsters that large families were once valued for.

Interestingly, studies indicate that two or three children is considered the ideal number by the great majority of people in all socioeconomic and ethnic groups. Many, however, have more children than they want, because of lack of access to effective means of birth control, or failure for one reason or another to use a reliable method regularly and as directed. Thus, some couples are in essence denied a choice; others take chances. One study indicated that 75 percent of women with large families had not wanted their last pregnancy. Many studies show that the burden of having unwanted children falls more heavily upon the poor than the well-to-do. All too often, poor women cannot afford effective contraceptives or do not have access to the kind of medical supervision that their proper use requires. All too often, also, poor women feel that available birth control programs are aimed at preventing them from having *any* children, not simply unwanted children. Changing this state of affairs will require concerted effort by citizens and medical personnel who are sensitive to the feelings of the poor, especially the poor who are members of minority groups.

The "Pill"

Properly used, birth control pills afford virtually 100 percent protection against pregnancy. A doctor's prescription is needed to purchase them. A month's supply costs around three dollars. They work by altering a woman's hormonal balance in order to prevent ovulation; that is, to prevent her ovaries from releasing an egg each month as they would normally do.

The pill was developed out of the knowledge that women do not ovulate when they are pregnant, because of hormonal changes that occur in the body following conception. Birth control pills simulate the hormonal conditions that exist during pregnancy. The pills are of two kinds: combination pills that contain both progestin and estrogen, and sequential pills in which initial doses of estrogen are followed by some progestin.

Both types are taken orally. Beginning usually on the fifth day after the onset of menstruation, a woman takes one pill a day for 20 or 21 days. For as long as she is taking the pill, her menstrual cycle is regularized;

her period starts a day or two after she has completed taking her allotted series of pills. It is extremely important, however, that she take a pill each day during the required time. Skipping a day, even if she takes two pills twenty-four hours later, may allow ovulation to occur and thus make it possible for her to conceive. For this reason, women using the pill are advised to keep some other form of contraceptive handy—a diaphragm or a supply of condoms—and use it as a back-up measure during the remainder of any month during which they forget to take their pill one day.

Aside from its effectiveness, the pill is an appealing method of birth control because it is easy to use and dissociates contraception from the act of having intercourse. When a woman is ready to become pregnant, she simply stops taking the pill and, except in rare instances, she is ovulating regularly within a month or two.

But How Safe Is It?

Although oral contraception was first greeted as the "perfect" solution to family planning, some questions about its safety, especially if used throughout a woman's reproductive years, have since been raised. Statistics indicate that there is a significantly higher incidence of blood-clotting problems (thrombophlebitis and pulmonary embolism) in women using the pill than in women the same age not using it. Still, the mortality rate from such problems among pill users appears to be very low, about 8 per 200,000, which is less than the mortality rate associated with pregnancy. Even so, women with a history of circulatory problems should certainly not use the pill. When a woman goes to a doctor for a prescription for an oral contraceptive, the doctor is supposed to take a careful medical history, in addition to giving a thorough medical examination. Both should be insisted upon.

There is no evidence to date that using the pill makes a woman more susceptible to breast cancer. In regard to cervical cancer, the statistics are more ambiguous. Some studies indicate that there may be a slightly higher incidence of such cancers among women who use the pill. However, this kind of cancer has a cure rate of approximately 100 percent when diagnosed in its early stages. Thus women using the pill who go to their doctors every six months for checkups, as they are supposed to do, may actually have less to fear from cervical cancer than do women who have a "Pap smear" test (the standard test for cervical cancer) less frequently.

In addition to the possible risks mentioned, the pill may produce certain unpleasant side effects in some users. Some women complain of nausea, though this usually disappears after a few months. Others experience breast enlargement and tenderness, annoying vaginal discharge or vaginal itching, periodic "bloating," weight gain that they are unable to control, or tension similar to premenstrual tension. Individual differences enter in markedly. Often an astute physican can eliminate all, or nearly all, the unpleasantness of which a woman complains by prescribing another brand of pills. The various brands affect different women differently. But occasionally switching brands does not help, and a woman and her doctor may conclude that some drawback, such as weight gain or nervous tension, makes it desirable for her to give up oral contraception.

Because the pill is relatively new, we do not know what its long-term risks may be, or whether, for example, a woman should make it her choice of contraception throughout her reproductive years. Many women are understandably nervous about altering their hormonal balance over a long period of time. More research is needed to give us the answer. Some young mothers now using the pill say that after they have had the children they want, they intend to be sterilized, have their tubes tied.

It is quite possible that the next few years will see the development of a form of contraception that is as effective as sterilization or the pill and more appealing than either. Meanwhile, on balance, the benefits of oral contraception appear to outweigh all its possible risks and other drawbacks. Having good medical supervision is a must, though. It keeps the risks minimal and usually enables a woman to avoid the more unpleasant side effects.

The IUD

The intrauterine device is a delicate, flexible "loop" or "coil," generally made of plastic, which is inserted through the cervical opening into a woman's uterus or womb. Insertion and removal must be done by a doctor. For as long as the device is in place, it affords almost complete (about 98 percent) protection against pregnancy. A woman continues to menstruate normally. When she is ready to have a baby, she simply has the device removed.

It is not known exactly how the IUD works. Prob-

197

ably an egg can become fertilized, but it is somehow prevented from nesting in the womb's lining and developing further.

This kind of "one-shot" approach to contraception —once the IUD is inserted, you are protected for as many months or years as it remains in place—has an obvious appeal. Again, however, there are drawbacks for some women. On the whole, the IUD is not suitable for women who have never been pregnant, especially if they are under twenty. In some women, it causes cramps or bleeding severe enough that the device must be removed. (Most women have some side effects for the first few months.) It is estimated that this happens in 10 to 15 percent of cases. Somewhat less frequently, the IUD is expelled spontaneously, that is, comes out of itself. If this occurs without a woman's knowledge, she is, of course, subject to becoming pregnant. To guard against this eventuality, IUDs today are equipped with a fine nylon thread that extends through the mouth of the womb into the vagina, so that a woman can check to make certain that the device is still in place.

There are no aftereffects on a woman's womb once the IUD has been removed. Other things being equal, she is as likely to become pregnant after using the device as she was before. In the rare cases in which pregnancy occurs despite the presence of an IUD, there is no evidence that the resulting infant will suffer any abnormality. After the baby is born, the IUD is delivered along with the placenta.

For the woman who can retain an IUD, it is a very easy, inexpensive, and almost foolproof method of contraception.

The Diaphragm with Spermicidal Jelly or Cream

The diaphragm is a shallow cuplike device of rubber with a thick springy edge, designed to fit snugly at the far end of the vagina, holding a spermicidal agent over the cervical opening and preventing sperm from entering the womb. (See illustration.) When properly fitted by a physician, and used in conjunction with a spermicidal jelly or cream according to the physician's directions, it is very effective in preventing fertilization. Some authorities assert that the only "accidents" that occur with a diaphragm are the result of "human failure." Others consider the method only about 96 percent effective, at best.

Unquestionably, using a diaphragm correctly can be a bother, and couples may sometimes be tempted to take a chance. A woman must insert the diaphragm before having intercourse and leave it in place for at least six hours afterward. If intercourse is desired more than an hour after the diaphragm has been put in place, its position should be checked and additional jelly or cream inserted. The fit of the diaphragm should be checked by the doctor who prescribed it two or three months after a woman is initially fitted. Refitting is also necessary after she has a baby. Normally a diaphragm holds up for several years, but it should be replaced if the rubber shows any signs of weakness.

From all this, it is evident that a couple need to be highly motivated in order to make the most of the protection that a diaphragm can afford. Still, the fact that it does not necessitate manipulating the body chemistry and has no side effects makes this method, in the opinion of many, worth the trouble it involves.

THE DIAPHRAGM

SPERMICIDAL JELLY

FLEXED FOR INSERTION

RUBBER-COATED
SPRING RIM

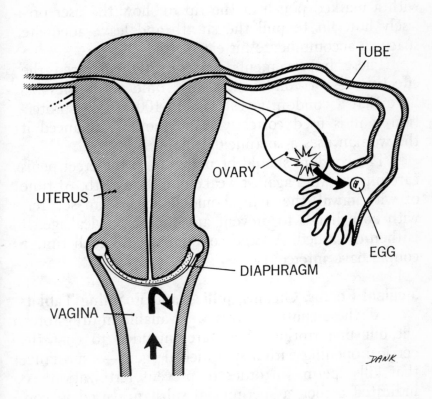

TUBE

OVARY

EGG

UTERUS

DIAPHRAGM

VAGINA

DANK

The Condom

Condoms can be bought in a drugstore. No prescription is needed to purchase them. Sometimes called a "rubber," the condom is a thin elastic sheath, several inches in length, intended to be pulled onto the man's erect penis just before intercourse and to contain his semen after he ejaculates, so that no sperm are deposited in the woman's vagina.

Condoms today are made of tougher material than they were some years ago. They are newly designed, too, with a marked pouch at the tip to show the user precisely how far to pull the sheath and leave adequate space to accommodate his ejaculate.

These improvements have greatly enhanced the effectiveness of condoms. Again, some authorities believe that a condom gives close to 100 percent protection if it is used correctly. Protection is enhanced if the woman uses a spermicidal foam.

The condom should be pulled onto the erect penis carefully, to ward against weakening the sheath. At time of withdrawal, the man should hold the rim securely with both hands to prevent any slipping or leakage. It is then discarded. A fresh condom is used each time a couple have intercourse.

Vaginal Foams, Creams, Jellies, and Foaming Tablets

All these contraceptives are available in drugstores, without prescription. They are intended to coat the cervical opening with a spermicidal agent—a substance that kills sperm—in order to prevent fertilization. As indicated earlier, a spermicidal substance used in conjunction with a diaphragm affords very good protec-

CONTRACEPTIVE FOAMS

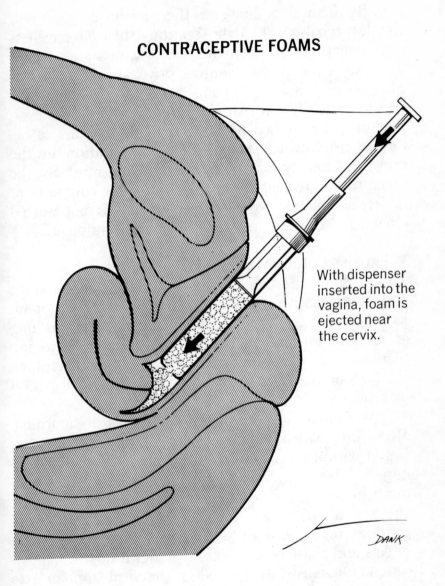

With dispenser inserted into the vagina, foam is ejected near the cervix.

DANK

tion. By themselves, however, these agents are considerably less reliable. The data regarding their effectiveness are conflicting, but even the foams, which are perhaps the best of this type of contraceptive, appear to be less than 80 percent sure. Foams have an advantage over creams and jellies in that they are not messy. However, they must be applied no more than thirty minutes before orgasm, which means that reapplication in the midst of foreplay may be necessary. Care must also be taken to ensure that the foam, from spray container or tablet, adequately covers the cervix and is not wasted elsewhere in the vagina. (See illustration on page 201.)

What the Future May Hold

Attempts are being made to develop once-a-month oral contraceptive pills and to perfect methods of injecting hormones that have a long-lasting effect, as long as several months. Another possibility may be to implant such hormones under the skin in a way that allows them to be released gradually over an extended period of time.

We already have what is known as a "morning-after" pill, which averts pregnancy when treatment is begun within a few days after sexual relations have occurred. This is useful in cases of rape and other incidents involving one isolated sexual encounter. However, the treatment, which involves taking large doses of estrogen orally, can cause extremely disagreeable side effects and must be carried out under a doctor's supervision. Obviously, this is not a practical approach to contraception for couples having intercourse regularly.

It is known that small amounts of progestin placed

in a woman's cervix will cause her cervical secretions to thicken sufficiently to prevent sperm from entering her womb. The amount of progestin needed seems to be so small that it produces only this local reaction and does not otherwise affect her body's functioning. Efforts are under way in two directions: to ascertain the precise dose of progestin needed to work, and to design a suitable device to hold it in place.

What about a contraceptive pill for men? This is also being investigated. Research has been centered mainly on interfering with spermatogenesis, the production of sperm. Some promising leads have had to be abandoned because the experimental pill produced proved incompatible with the consumption of alcohol.

Meanwhile, researchers continue to try to improve the contraceptives presently available. The dosage of hormones in oral contraceptives has been steadily lowered ever since the pills came on the market, without reducing their effectiveness. Still further progress may come in this direction, which would lead to further reduction of unpleasant side effects and possible risks.

Rhythm Method

For couples who have religious scruples against using other methods of birth control, the rhythm method, which requires abstaining from intercourse during a woman's "fertile period"—the period just before and after she ovulates—can now be practiced with somewhat more hope of success than formerly, though the failure rate is still discouragingly high. The crucial factor in the rhythm method is, of course, to determine exactly when a woman will ovulate—and this is important to couples who *want* to have a baby, as well as to those who do not. A woman is fertile for no more than two days before the ovum, or egg, leaves the ovary (two days being the maximum length of time that sperm are capable of fertilization after ejaculation) and for no more than two days following ovulation (that being the maximum time that the ovum remains fresh enough to be fertilized).

Most women ovulate around the middle of their menstrual cycle, or about fourteen days after the onset of menstruation. But that statistic is of no help in avoiding or fostering conception. Each woman has her own brief fertile period, which may vary from month to month. The time of ovulation can be determined with impressive exactitude if a woman has the patience and knowledge needed to keep a daily chart of her basal body temperature, a technique described in detail in *A Woman's Choice: A Guide to Contraception, Fertility, Abortion, and Menopause* by Robert H. Glass, M.D., and Nathan G. Kase, M.D.

A woman's temperature rises detectably at the time of ovulation. (See illustration.) To avoid pregnancy, however, or to become pregnant, a woman needs to know two days before she ovulates that this event is impending. The Basal Temperature Chart may offer a clue to this, too. Generally a woman's temperature drops a day or so before the rise associated with ovulation, but this warning probably comes too late to enable a couple to avoid conception with any degree of certainty. More help is provided by the fact that the chemistry of a woman's cervical secretions changes several days before ovulation. Nature makes her reproduc-

THERMAL SHIFT
GRAPH OF BASAL BODY TEMPERATURE DURING AN AVERAGE MENSTRUAL PERIOD.

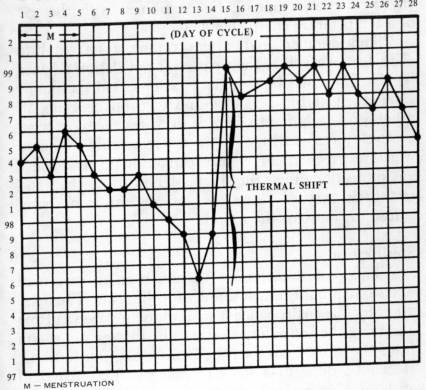

M — MENSTRUATION

tive tract more hospitable to sperm. The cervical secretions become more watery, abundant, and alkaline, providing an environment that prolongs the life of sperm and makes it easier for them to get through the mouth of the womb. Kits that enable a woman to test the chemical makeup of her cervical secretions, and in many cases determine accurately several days ahead that she is due to ovulate, are available in drugstores. These kits do not make the rhythm approach to birth control anywhere near foolproof, but combined with the use of a temperature chart, they help.

Some women find, after keeping a temperature chart for a year, that their pattern of ovulation is quite regular. They may be tempted to assume that they know when their fertile period is and give up checking in other ways each month. This is risky, for the most regular cycle occasionally changes unpredictably. Women who are irregular, of course, cannot hope to achieve any protection unless they keep a temperature chart and test their cervical secretions—or abstain from intercourse for most of the month.

Sterilization

This procedure can be performed on either a man or a woman but is much simpler for the male. The operation for the male, called a vasectomy, involves cutting and tying the vas deferens—the tube that carries sperm from the storage area to the penis. (See illustration.) It can be done in a doctor's office in less than half an hour. Cutting and tying a woman's Fallopian tubes is major surgery, requiring an abdominal incision under anesthesia. (See illustration.)

Neither operation affects the hormonal functioning of the person involved. Sexual desire and performance need not be in any way affected. The result is simply, in the case of the male, to eliminate sperm from the ejaculate, and, in the case of the female, to prevent eggs from being fertilized. Both operations are sometimes reversible—in perhaps half of all cases for men, less

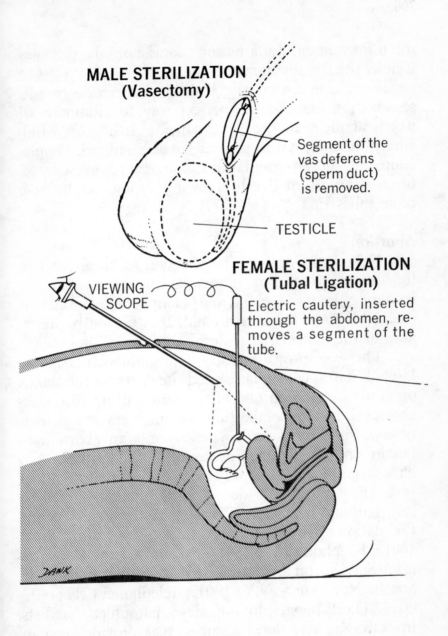

MALE STERILIZATION
(Vasectomy)

Segment of the
vas deferens
(sperm duct)
is removed.

TESTICLE

FEMALE STERILIZATION
(Tubal Ligation)

VIEWING
SCOPE

Electric cautery, inserted
through the abdomen, re-
moves a segment of the
tube.

DANIK

often for women. But a person should not take this step if he or she has any lingering doubts.

For a couple who have had the children they want, sterilization may be the perfect way to eliminate all worry about unwanted pregnancies. It is sure, and, when the man is the partner to be sterilized, simple. More and more young fathers today are having a vasectomy as an alternative to allowing their wives to have their tubes tied.

Abortion

Nobody advocates legal abortion as an alternative to contraception. But numerous thoughtful persons, including many doctors and clergymen, consider it preferable to an unwanted child. It is obviously preferable to the dangers that illegal abortion poses.

The widespread practice of illegal abortion in the United States, which has caused the death of thousands of women, has been one factor contributing to the recent push to reform abortion laws in many states. It is now possible for a woman who wants an abortion to obtain one legally in this country, though she may have to go out of her state to do so. Information about costs and referral to a doctor or hospital is offered by two national agencies: Planned Parenthood—World Population, 810 Seventh Avenue, New York, N.Y. 10019, telephone (212) 541-7800; and Clergy Consultation Service on Abortion, 55 Washington Square, South, New York, N.Y. 10012, telephone (212) 477-0034. The Bibliography includes a pamphlet that lists, by state and city, local agencies that provide such information and referrals.

The earlier in pregnancy that an abortion is done, the better. Some states permit an abortion to be performed through the twenty-fourth week, but many doctors refuse to perform the operation after the twentieth week except in very special circumstances. The optimal time is through the tenth week, that is, up to the time when a woman is due to miss her third period. Up to this point, abortion, when done legally, is extremely safe, safer than normal delivery.

Early abortions are of two types: the D & C (dilatation and curettage), which is done under anesthesia and involves scraping the lining of the womb clean; and the Suction Method, in which a small tube is inserted in the uterus and draws the pregnancy out. Neither of these methods usually requires an overnight stay in the hospital or clinic where it is done.

Later abortions are more complicated and generally require a stay of two or more days in the hospital where they are performed.

Treatment for Infertility

A couple should seek treatment for infertility together, for a very simple reason: it is much quicker, easier, and less expensive to evaluate a man's fertility than to evaluate a woman's. Most gynecologists can do this, though if the husband requires treatment, a urologist will be consulted. If your own doctor does not handle fertility problems, he will recommend a specialist, or a clinic, that does.

The evaluation of a man's fertility is made through microscopic examination of a semen specimen, ordinarily obtained by masturbation. The specimen must be examined within two hours after ejaculation. The doctor needs to know whether the man's sperm count and the number of abnormal-appearing sperm are within the normal range.

Another test done early in the course of infertility treatment, because it is simple, is examination of the woman's cervical secretions following intercourse. This reveals the extent to which sperm can survive in her reproductive tract and indicates whether or not her secretions are unusually hostile to them.

Testing to see if a woman is ovulating normally, and if not why not, takes time. The doctor will check on ovulation by having her keep a basal body temperature chart (See page 205) for several months and perhaps also by performing an endometrial biopsy—removing a bit of tissue from the lining of the womb and examining it under a microscope. This not only tells whether ovulation is occurring but also reveals whether progesterone production is adequate. Tests will be made to determine if the Fallopian tubes are open and healthy so that the ovum is accessible to sperm and the fertilized egg could make its way, at a normal rate of speed, to the womb.

A very few women cannot conceive because they are allergic to their husband's sperm. (This is not the same as having cervical secretions that are hostile to sperm.) There is now a way to test for such allergy, and it can be treated.

If you wish more information about the many tests available to pinpoint infertility problems, consult the Bibliography. Improved testing has probably contributed as much as advances in treatment to the ability of modern medical specialists to help parents have the children they want.

The most publicized recent advance in treatment has been the development of "fertility drugs," notably Clomid. Clomid, which is taken in pill form under a doctor's supervision, stimulates ovulation, apparently by causing the pituitary gland to produce more of the hormones a woman needs to ovulate. Though Clomid is much less potent currently than it originally was, a woman still runs the risk of multiple births when she takes it. Clomid has also been used to treat men with a fertility problem, but it is not always successful in improving the quality of semen.

There are other recent approaches to hormonal therapy for women. Commercially prepared hormones may be given in doses that approximate what nature intended, to trigger ovulation. Since much has been learned in recent years about hormonal functioning in both men and women, doctors are better able to detect and compensate for an individual's lacks in this area. Some doctors have reported that up to 70 percent of their women infertility patients treated in this manner became pregnant. As with Clomid therapy, however, a woman's ovaries may sometimes be "overstimulated," and multiple births can occur.

"Fertility drugs" are an exciting development in the treatment of infertility. As this type of therapy becomes increasingly refined with time, it should involve fewer drawbacks for women and perhaps offer more help to men. It will never be a cure-all, however, since there are problems, such as malfunctioning tubes, with which it cannot help. When a couple seek help from a competent fertility specialist, they should be prepared to accept his decision that he has done all that can be done. When that point has been reached, they would be wise to set a deadline for themselves, after which they will give up working at trying to conceive and investigate adoption or devote their energies to achieving other satisfactions in life.

Adoption

Professionals who work with families agree that parents should consult a licensed adoption agency if they want to adopt a child. This is not just a matter of "experts sticking up for each other." Although non-agency adoptions sometimes work out beautifully, and agencies occasionally make mistakes (in addition to requiring a lengthy investigation), agency adoptions have a number of advantages: (1) prospective parents receive counseling about child-rearing and the problems that adoptive parents are likely to encounter; (2) agencies are prepared to deal with such eventualities as an unexpected pregnancy after a couple have been promised a child; (3) agencies offer parents support and advice during the early months when they are adjusting to their child; (4) the natural mother is less likely to change her mind and try to reclaim the baby when an adoption is handled by an agency; and (5) agency adoptions, even if the agency is a private one, are on the whole considerably less expensive.

Unfortunately, there is today a growing black market in the adoption field. This is because the supply of adoptable white babies has shrunk markedly in recent years.

One of the largest United States private agencies, which in 1968 arranged 1,903 adoptions, expected in 1971 to arrange less than half that number, or 888. As of June 1971 the agency stopped accepting applications from couples who want only white infants.

This trend is thought to have three main causes: the increased availability of contraceptives, especially the Pill; liberalized abortion laws; and a dramatic increase in the number of unmarried girls who decide to keep their babies. At the same time, the demand for babies appears to be increasing, partly because a number of couples feel that, in view of the population explosion, they should have no more than two children of their own and adopt any more that they want.

One good feature of all this is that many children who a few years ago would have been slated to spend their lives in institutions or foster homes are now being adopted. Interracial adoptions are on the rise, as the supply of babies of minority-group origin still greatly exceeds the demand for them by couples of like origin. What evidence we have to date indicates that interracial adoptions are as successful as any other kind, for everybody concerned. But there is a lack of long-term research into this.

Older children and children with handicaps are also being adopted in increasing numbers. There have always been a few such adoptions. One recent study of a number of them *Adopting Older Children*, by Alfred Kadushin, indicates that here, too, the success rate, judged in terms of parental satisfaction, compares very favorably with that of more conventional adoptions. When older children are adopted, they tend on the whole to "show gratitude and not complain," and to "try hard to be good"—to quote some parents surveyed in the foregoing study. This is understandable; such children have tasted what *not* having a family means. It does, however, point up the fact that parents who adopt older children, especially from an institution, may need to help the child feel comfortable about expressing normal irritation and resentment without fear that this might jeopardize his relationship with his adoptive parents. Couples considering this kind of adoption (and perhaps interracial adoption also) should be certain that they are motivated by concern for the child's welfare, and not just narcissism. Children deserve the right to be thoroughgoing ingrates occasionally and not have to appreciate us all of the time.

Young marrieds today are showing a heartening concern about having only as many children as they, and the world, can accommodate adequately. This, combined with their rejection of pigeonholing people according to race, should mean that in the decade to come there will be fewer unwanted babies and that every child born will have a better chance of enjoying the advantages that should be the birthright of all children.

11

Our Needs In Perspective

I<small>N BECOMING PARENTS</small> we do not cease to be people, with lives of our own to lead and needs which, whether we are male or female, cannot be totally satisfied simply through having and rearing children. That statement is a truism. Yet many parents feel uncomfortable with the idea that their own needs are always important, should always be taken into account, and sometimes deserve to take precedence over some of their children's needs.

Partly, this is because many of us are imbued with the notion that it is selfish to pay any attention to our own self-interest. That is untrue. One of the basic tenets of psychology is that unless a person's own needs are adequately met he is not capable of properly assessing and ministering to the needs of another.

This principle was examined earlier in the discussion of how children learn to respect the rights of others. It applies to us as well as to our children. If we continually do violence to our own self-interest, our children will be made to pay for it in one way or another. Often in middle-class circles children pay through being saddled with an almost unbearable burden of guilt. In other circles, when parents are insufficiently fulfilled personally, the young may be beaten viciously, or their care may be relegated almost exclusively to hired help.

Another and perhaps even more important reason that we frequently hesitate to weigh our own interests as carefully as we should is that we somehow feel that meeting our own needs adequately will inevitably result in slighting our children's. This is also fundamentally fallacious, the result of viewing the interests of parents and their children as being diametrically opposed. Actually they often go hand in hand. When conflicts arise, the interests of one party do not usually have to be totally overridden in order to ensure the well-being of the other. A variety of adjustments and compromises are nearly always possible.

The Trap of Thinking in Terms of Opposites

It is not surprising that we often think in terms of opposing extremes rather than in the round. The adversary approach is endemic in our culture. It does not really come naturally to us to size up all the possible options available to us in a given situation.

Linguists have commented on the extent to which Western languages, unlike Eastern ones, both reflect and encourage a tendency to think in terms of opposites, or mutually exclusive choices. Either/or. You can't have your cake and eat it too. He who is not for me is against me. Take sides. Crossing the Rubicon. All or nothing.

The more skillfully we avoid this way of sizing up our options, the better off we and our children will be. In rearing our children and in leading our own lives we must, of course, constantly make decisions. But each decision is only one step in a very long journey. It will shift us away from some possibilities, at least temporarily, yet at the same time it also opens up new ones. Before making any decision, we should survey the full circle of moves available to us. We need not lock ourselves into viewing the situation as affording only a few mutually exclusive choices. And after the step has been taken, and our perspective has been changed by that much, it is again important to survey the full circle of moves available to us.

How Our Way of Viewing Problems Matters

There are times when our children's needs must clearly take precedence over our own. A sick child needs attention, regardless of how tired we may be. Yet, even here, if we define the problem accurately as seeing that the child has the attention he needs, we may discover that the possibilities for handling it are more numerous than would appear at first glance. The mother of a three-year-old reports:

George had a very rough case of chicken pox, and I was going out of my mind because my husband was away on business and there was nobody to spell me at night. When Judy, my best friend, called, it must have been evident what a state I was in. She said she would get her mother to stay with her kids and would be over shortly to take care of George so I could get some sleep. I protested, but she insisted. She said she'd had chicken pox and George liked her and wouldn't I do the same for her? She arrived within an hour with a note from her mother to me, saying Judy was to stay as long as needed—everything under control at the other end. Judy stayed two days, until George was comfortable enough so I could manage alone. As a result of that experience, Judy and I started a cooperative baby-sitting setup among our friends which covers emergencies as well as the usual. Like our group knows which parents have had which children's diseases, and we will take on each other's crying infants if one of us is desperate for sleep. The men suggested including help with crying infants, and that has been interesting. Sometimes having a new person aboard really calms things down, and some of our best infant soothers are fathers.

Often it is in the financial area that our children's needs conflict with ours. Willie's need for orthodontic care obviously takes priority over our plans for a second honeymoon. But does meeting his need for braces really exclude meeting our need for a vacation alone? Have we considered the possibility of having Willie treated in a clinic rather than by a private orthodontist? And have we considered all the possible ways in which we might manage a second honeymoon fairly inexpensively, including arranging for our children to visit relatives while we stay home? Another mother says:

Bill and I had been saving for several years to go to Europe together the summer of our fifteenth wedding anniversay. Bill would be due for four weeks' vacation for the first time, and his parents had offered to keep our three kids for us. Then the winter before we were due to go, Bill's father had a heart attack and our Jill had to have an appendectomy. Our plans were blown sky high. Jill's surgery took a big bite out of our savings, and we knew Bill's parents shouldn't take on our kids even if they offered to. We also knew that with Bill's father not entirely recovered, it wasn't the time to leave the country. We were pretty disappointed, and our friends and the people Bill works with knew it. One of Bill's co-workers mentioned that he had taken a very large house on the beach for the summer. It was really too expensive and too big for his family, and he was looking for somebody to share it. He suggested that if we went in together on the house for the season and we got along with each other's kids, maybe we could swap off caring for the lot so that each couple could go away on a vacation alone for a week or so. We took him up and it worked. Our kids adored being at the beach all summer, and Bill and I spent two great weeks alone together on a camping trip in the mountains. I can't say it was like going to Europe for Bill and me, but it was a better vacation for all of us than I'd thought we could work out.

It Is Not Always So Easy

There is no question but that sometimes conflicts of interest between parent and child cannot be resolved, or even alleviated much, through tickling them with all the available feathers. Cooperative arrangements for caring for children, for example, are not a possible option for us if we do not know some other parents fairly well or if our child is not agreeable to such arrangements. Then, too, some parents simply do not find the idea appealing. If we are not by temperament suited to being involved in cooperative enterprises, we certainly should not push ourselves in this direction, at least not until we have exhausted all other options.

As for money, there are times when it simply runs out. We are left with no leeway for juggling expenditures. Everyday necessities consume all we have to spend.

In large matters and in small, parents often have to make sacrifices for their children. Generally we do it automatically, because we care about our children. Their well-being and their happiness matter more to us than our personal comfort. We do not expect them to notice and be grateful for all the ways in which we extend ourselves to meet their needs, though, of course, the occasional expressions of gratitude that we do get are heartwarming.

Sacrifices made in this spirit do not really violate our self-interest. Like the experience of walking the floor in the middle of the night with an unhappy baby and feeling him finally relax in our arms and drop off to sleep, they are their own reward. It is only when we begin constantly to resent our lot, when meeting our

222

obligations as parents is continually felt as more of a
burden than a pleasure, as inimical to our personal
fulfillment, that the atmosphere becomes tainted and
children and parents alike suffer.

Avoiding Unnecessary Resentment

Such a state of affairs is often due to demanding
more of ourselves than is really required, or under-
estimating our children's ability to adjust their needs
to accommodate ours. A six-year-old, for example, does
not have an inalienable right to skip rope or bounce
a ball in the hall if it gets on our nerves. Granted, the
activity is pleasurable for him and does not harm the
hall and does not get on every parent's nerves. But if
it bothers us, we had better say so, not grit our teeth
and suffer in silence.

As indicated all along, children whose rights are
appropriately respected usually show surprising ability
to heed a peremptory, "That noise is driving me nuts.
Please find something else to do." Or, "Get those toys
out from underfoot PLEASE." At an early age they can
accept the fact that there are limits to our ability to
tolerate noise, messiness, and such. They may not empathize with our limits. Grown-ups are a strange breed to
children. Our ideas about what is important often seem
peculiar to them. Yet the child is usually willing to
honor his elders' peculiar needs if they are not too
numerous and are clearly enunciated, and if he is
thanked for it, and if he knows that his own idiosyn-
crasies are respected even when they cannot be honored.
That is a lot of "ifs," but they are all important.

In middle-class households a common cause of

much parental irritation is the fact that children have a way of standing around and watching grown-ups work without feeling any urge to lend a hand. Wrapped up in regaling us with tales of their latest comings and goings, they may possibly step out of the path of the vacuum cleaner without being asked, but it will seldom occur to them to lift a finger to move a chair or any other piece of furniture. We tend to suffer our exasperation in silence because we want very much to be privy to their doings, and we do not need their help that much. They, in their turn, do not really comprehend why we become somewhat short-tempered. They know that we like them to tell us about their affairs, don't we? They have not been taught the lesson that less privileged children learn very early: Stay out of the way when grown-ups are working hard; otherwise you will be yelled at or roped into helping.

"Damn it," a father said to his eleven-year-old daughter who was accompanying her parents around their home, chattering happily, as her father and mother set about installing speakers for their newly acquired stereo, "don't you realize how infuriating it is to watch somebody taking it easy when you're working your head off?"

"Damn it," the girl responded with equal heat, "if you want me to help or to shut up, why don't you just ask?" In the ensuing conversation, the parents admitted that they should have expressed their feelings honestly right away, should have told the girl that while they wanted very much to hear what she had to say, this was not the time for an extended conversation. And the child admitted that it was understandable, once you stopped to think about it, that people would get annoyed at having you standing around running off at the mouth when they were hard at work. She had never before thought about it.

Middle-class children frequently are confused about when and how to lend a hand, and how to avoid irritating us when we are busy and their help is not needed. Too often, we fail to give them the specific guidance they need in this area. This does *them* a disservice, as well as ourselves, for it fosters habits of behavior that may make them seem spoiled in the eyes of many people.

Overprotection

Another source of unnecessary parental resentment is our natural tendency to spare our children many of the worries that we wrestle with. There are times, of course, when this is justified. Children should not be burdened with all our adult concerns about matters of health, finances, and the future. When we are deeply worried, however, it is wise to share this fact with our children in a fashion that is suited to their age and understanding.

For example, if a husband's job is in jeopardy, the strain that he and his wife are under will probably communicate itself to children as young as six or thereabouts. They sense that their parents are somehow different, harder to get along with. It may actually come as a relief to them to be told, "Daddy is worried about his job. He's afraid he may have to get another one. This makes him act cross sometimes, and me too. It isn't going to be like this forever, but we want you to know why we're upset, so you won't think it's your fault."

We need to remember that our children, even after they reach adolescence, think of us as being far more powerful and able to cope with the world and to protect them than we actually are. They simply do not worry, as we do, about what could happen if Daddy or Mommy lost their job. They assume that we will somehow continue to manage in the way that we have heretofore. This is just as well.

They can make allowances, often quite touchingly, for our behavior if they have been informed that we are under stress. But when no explanation whatsoever is offered, they tend to become difficult or withdrawn in response to our moodiness, and perhaps feel guilty about the situation, thinking they have brought it on somehow. This adds to the stress we are under already.

In sharing the truth with our children, we try not to frighten them or worry them needlessly. We withhold information that they cannot handle, though without resorting to lies. Certainly a father does not tell his children that, given his age, he is afraid he will not be able to find another job as good as the one he now has. If they question him about his plans, as young children may do, out of curiosity more than real anxiety, an "Oh, I'll find something" will settle the matter reassuringly and is an honest declaration of intent. Similarly, if a member of the family is gravely ill, a child has to be told the person is ill, so that he can handle our tension. However, he does not need to know how serious the illness is. If he asks if the person will get well, and if the circumstances demand that we be reassuring (which would certainly be true in the case of a parent's or a sibling's illness), we can respond that everything is being done to ensure this and that we do not want him to worry. Again, the child's faith in our power to move mountains works to our advantage. Some such statement usually reassures the child under eight or nine and many older children. If it is apparent that a youngster, because of his age or temperament, still worries, we allow him to share his pain and anxiety with us, answering his questions honestly, though putting the best face possible on matters. By treating him as an equal, we let him experience at least the comfort of closeness with us.

Leveling appropriately with our children about what the family is up against is healthy for us and for them. It enables us to "ventilate" some of our feelings, so that pressure does not build up to an intolerable point. It guards against the possibility that our children may feel unnecessarily to blame for tensions that they detect in us. Finally, it encourages our children to face reality and to function as responsible members of the family who are expected to contribute what they can to the well-being of the household.

Trying to insulate our children from life as it is seldom makes any lasting contribution to their happiness and may seriously interfere with their maturing. As emphasized previously, we do not have to create artificial challenges in order to help them grow up. Life itself offers real challenges enough, even for the most fortunate. However, when challenges do arise, our children should be expected to face them to the extent of their ability.

The Temptation to Live Through Our Children

If parents do not take their own personal needs sensibly into account, they also greatly increase the ever-present risk that they will look to their children to provide them vicariously with the emotional satisfactions that every person craves. All of us identify to some extent with our children. We are buoyed by their successes and saddened by their failures. This is as it should be, so long as at the same time we maintain a healthy awareness that our offsprings' successes and failures are indeed theirs, not ours.

Self-fulfilled parents have that awareness. When Jane runs for president of her high school and makes it, we share her elation, but we do not see it as a victory that we have somehow personally wrought and can take credit for. It is her doing. Likewise, if she loses, we do our best to help her be philosophical about it. But we do not take the defeat personally, as if the outcome had depended on us and in some way diminishes us.

Being proud of or sad with our children is one thing. Trying to live through them is quite another. We have all known parents so determined that their children be or do what they themselves were never able to be or do that they run roughshod over the children's own feelings and interests. Parents who never went to college may become so obsessed with having their children go that they are blind to what kind of education would be best for the individual child concerned. A father who was never good at athletics may be determined that his son become an athlete, regardless of the son's interests. A mother who was never particularly popular may push her daughter socially, bent on having the child gain the kind of recognition the mother always wanted, even though the child is drawn to more introspective friends and activities. Some of the pressure that young people are under to gain admission to prestigious colleges is undoubtedly the result of parental needs rather than the needs of the young.

Of course, children are also often pressured to follow in the footsteps of parents who have achieved obvious success in one area or another. The mother who was a great belle pushes her daughter to be the same; the doctor father presses his son to go into medicine. Although it is natural to want one's children to do what one has found satisfying, empathic parents stop pushing when the child resists or shows differing habits. If pushing persists in the face of determined resistance, here, too, it is apparent that although the parents may seem to be self-fulfilled persons, they view their children as extensions of themselves rather than separate individuals with lives of their own to live. The parents cannot feel truly successful unless their children achieve success as the parents define it. A variety of factors may contribute to this, including on the part of one or both parents a limited concept of what constitutes the good life. The net result, however, is to place children in the unfair position of being instruments through which their parents attempt to achieve needed satisfactions. The parents should be paddling their own canoes.

Our children need us to guide them, to give them the full benefit of the wisdom that experience ordinarily confers, to point out the pitfalls of which the young are often unaware. But in the final analysis, our children must decide what they want to do with their lives. If we look appropriately to our own fulfillment as individuals, we are more likely to give our children their heads to the extent we should.

Fulfillment in Work

There are many men as well as women who view working with children as the most challenging and satisfying of all possible tasks. We have pediatricians and child therapists and teachers and full-time mothers who love their work and find it deeply fulfilling. Today there is a tendency in some circles to denigrate the job of full-time mother, unless a woman is being paid to mother children other than her own. This is as silly as the tendency not long ago to denigrate any mother who worked outside her home.

The only real problem about the job of full-time mother—if you like it, that is—is that unlike being a teacher, pediatrician, or such, it has a limited future. By the time you reach your prime, or earlier, you will be—perhaps *should* be is correct here—in the market for another job. Once all the children are in school for most of the day, they no longer require full-time maternal attention. If at that point a mother does not have some other interests to engage her energies, both she and her children may suffer.

Every woman has to resolve her need for fulfilling work in her own way. A wider range of choices is open to her now than ever before. More women than ever before are combining rearing children with holding down a full- or part-time job. More men are eager, not just willing, to share in all aspects of child care from

the moment their babies arrive on the scene, which
makes it easier for mothers to work. A growing number
of fathers are willing to arrange their working lives so
that they can take on the care of their children while
their wives secure professional training or get started in
a career. For the woman who does not need to work
for money, there is a greater variety of opportunities
to be involved in stimulating volunteer activities in the
community than ever before. Also, society at large is
more open to the idea of enabling women in their
middle years who have reared their children to return
to school or find jobs that utilize skills learned through
running a home and bringing up children. On-the-job
training is coming back into vogue.

Nevertheless, if a woman wants to work, or has to
work, when her children are small, she is likely to find
the going rough occasionally. The major concern of
most working mothers is the kind of care their children
receive in their absence.

Then, too, as one working mother says, "Don't tell
me it's the *quality* of the time you spend with your
children rather than the amount that's important. Both
are important." Working mothers with small children,
and even school-age ones, had best accept the fact that
they will be pulled in conflicting directions from time
to time. But that also happens if a mother stays at
home. Increasingly, professional people who work with
children and families are coming to the common-sense
conclusion that if a woman really wants to work, she
and her children will be better off if she does, and that
society should assume the responsibility for providing
first-rate facilities for the care of children of all working

mothers during whatever hours the mother is at her job. This may soon come about, though the care will probably not be free for all mothers, as some groups have urged. Still, it should be relatively inexpensive compared to employing household help.

What about a father's right to fulfillment in work? It is becoming increasingly apparent that many men with jobs that pay very well are not happy in their work. They feel locked into their jobs by the need to support their families (and themselves) in the fashion to which all have grown accustomed. This, too, seems to be changing somewhat. The number of young men who are more concerned about how interesting and socially useful a job is than about how much it will pay appears to be growing. Some corporations are sending out long-haired recruiters to college campuses in the hope of influencing greater numbers of the better-qualified graduates to consider going to work for them. One such recruiter says, "You just wind up listening to guys trying to persuade you to go into elementary school teaching, or police work. *Police work.*"

The crumbling of stereotyped attitudes toward work (or anything else) is a heartening sign. If it enables more members of our society, regardless of sex, race, or class, to arrive at more innovative ways of reconciling their personal interests, their financial needs, and their children's needs, society as well as the families concerned will be strengthened.

Fulfillment in Marriage

Some members of the women's liberation movement are warning women nowadays that children can

interfere with having a satisfying relationship with a man. This is not news. Psychiatrists have been pointing out for years the ways in which children test the strength of a marriage and the emotional maturity of both partners. They have always cautioned against having children in the hope of saving a shaky marriage.

Nevertheless, if a marriage is sound to begin with, children can strengthen the bonds between a man and a woman and add new dimensions to their relationship. The birth of a baby is a kind of emotional high-water mark, like falling in love. Mature partners who have shared these two experiences are linked by bonds capable of withstanding a great deal of rough weather.

Yet children can put a strain on the personal relationship between man and wife in two ways. They consume a great deal of the time and energy of both parents, especially during the child's early years. In addition, their presence tends to reactivate any problems that either parent once had with his or her own parents or siblings—and all of us once had some.

About the matter of time, husband and wife will have to learn to budget it carefully, so that they still have time to be themselves and time for each other, as well as good times with their children.

The sexual relationship is a crucial factor in the health of a marriage, though partners who have earned each other's devotion have much in addition to hold them together.

The so-called sexual revolution of today has not really taught us anything about sex that was not known already. There is nothing new about sex outside marriage, or the desire to experience unrestrained sexual pleasure without guilt. Available research makes it clear that the vast majority of men and women, including the sexually "liberated," still hope to find sexual fulfillment within the context of some kind of continuing relationship. Couples should not need a marriage counselor or psychiatrist to tell them that this happens only if both persons involved give careful, considerate attention to making it happen—at least if the relationship lasts any length of time.

Yet, there is clinical evidence that many sophisticated young men and women who start off together with excellent sex let it dwindle away gradually because both keep waiting for lightning to strike, as it did constantly when they were first getting to know each other. Lightning *can* strike surprisingly often, even after years of being married and rearing children. But not unless both partners carefully nurture the spark, through all the days and nights when there are babies to walk the floor with, toddlers to run after, preschoolers to be helped to get over their fear of the dark, homework to be supervised, bills that somebody has to earn the money to pay, teen-agers to sit down with at the oddest hours, when they just happen to show an inclination to let down their hair and talk, and talk, and talk, as if for the first time in their lives they thought we knew something they did not know.

A good long-term sexual relationship, like any work in progress, sometimes streaks ahead under its own steam. At other times it proceeds more prosaically. The artisan works at it faithfully, knowing that if he neglects it too often or for too long a spell the initial inspiration will be hard to recapture.

The presence of children can activate a parent's ancient history at any point in a marriage. A father feels jealous of his baby's claim on his wife's attention. A mother feels left out as she watches her husband and their teen-age son planning a fishing expedition together. Parents find themselves in competition with each other for the affection or admiration of a child— or in competition with their own youngster, striving not to be outdone in this, that, or the other. Petty. Childish. But we cannot help how we feel.

The minute there are more than two people in the family picture, our old reactions to being just one among several, rather than the favored one, are likely to be triggered. We may compete, or withdraw, be jealous, hurt, angry, whatever, not so much because of what is specifically being done to us in the present, but because the present setup hooks us into how we reacted to similar setups in the past. Parents who are aware of the subtle ways in which children can bring out in us the child we once were are in a better position to avoid relating immaturely to their children and to each other. They tell each other honestly when they feel hurt or left out or angry, and work things out in terms of what is going on now. The ghosts of the past are more likely to be laid if we cope with the present forthrightly. Again, we do not try to analyze each other, just be honest about what we are feeling.

Divorce

Some marriages cannot be made to work. Responsible persons generally find it difficult to break off any relationship that has once meant something. If the relationship is a marriage that involves children, breaking it up is even harder. However, it sometimes needs to be done. The weight of the evidence convincingly supports the idea that children are better able to cope with divorce than with living in a home where parents are hopelessly at odds.

This is not to say that divorce is easy for children. As with other difficult challenges, however, children can manage if they are given adequate support from adults who matter to them. It is important that they not feel somehow to blame for the divorce, and that parents not deliberately attempt to undermine each other's standing with their children.

Grandparents and other relatives can be enormously helpful to children when parents divorce. Being a part of an extended family reassures a child that come what may, somebody will take care of him lovingly. That can remove what is perhaps the greatest threat that divorce poses for children: the fear of being left without any loved and caring adult to look after them. A child can get over losing, partially or completely, someone he loves if others whom he loves remain reliably in the picture. A selective list of materials on divorce is included in the Bibliography.

One-parent Families

Attitudes toward the one-parent family appear to be changing. Many professionals are pointing out that it is the overall quality of a child's home life, not who rears him, that matters. A recent roundup of all available research on children reared by one parent indicates that they seem to turn out as emotionally healthy as children from intact families if the person who rears them is aware of their special needs. All children do need to have close ties with adults of both sexes, but opportunities can be found for a child with only one parent for some such ties outside the immediate family circle, if this need is understood.

One sign of changing attitudes is the fact that some respected adoption agencies now permit single persons, male as well as female, to adopt young children. Of course, a single parent may often be subjected to extra stress simply because she or he is solely responsible for meeting the everyday challenges of living with a child. When a child is in a balky mood, or wakes up in the night with a fever, two parents have more going for them than one. Financial strains on the one-parent family also tend to be more acute, and if the parent works, seeing that the child is at all times and under all conditions adequately looked after is more continually a worry than if there were two to share the responsibility.

Thus, while single parents can succeed as well as any if they understand their children's individual needs, they are more likely to require support from friends, relatives, and the community. In many instances, appropriate support from the community is not forthcoming, although outstanding exceptions are often found in black communities. Similar exceptions can also be found in the military services, where there is special sensitivity to the problems of women separated from their husbands for extended periods and required to function as single parents.

The emphasis throughout this book is on the kind of care that *all* children need. When developmental challenges, such as the preschooler's need to identify with members of his own sex, might pose special problems in a one-parent family, single parents are alerted to this possibility and to ways of handling the challenge in their particular circumstances.

Disappointments and Lasting Difficulties

No matter how fulfilled we are as individuals and how successfully we resist the temptation to live through our children, we will have our share of parental disappointments. There will be times when our children's choices are not what we hoped for, but we must accept their right to choose. Watching a youngster move in his own directions is occasionally quite painful (as well as often exhilarating), as it inevitably involves some learning through trial and error and some breaking away from our views and priorities. Yet such hurts need not be lasting if we keep open our lines of communication with our children and relate to them as individuals with lives of their own to lead.

Then there are the disappointments that nature deals us. These are harder for even the healthiest parents to handle. Brilliant parents sometimes have quite ordinary children; not all boys are big and strong; not all girls are pretty; some children are born with pronounced physical or mental handicaps.

There is a profound difference, of course, between having low-normal intelligence and being retarded. There is an equally big difference between being "plain" and being deaf. Yet a child of low-normal intelligence in a bright family and an ugly duckling in a handsome family can subject parents to lasting strains on the order of those felt by parents of many children designated as handicapped.

It is all very well to assert that we should not be so concerned about boys being big and strong, girls being pretty, and children of both sexes being "bright." Of course, as parents and as a society our goal should be simply to enable every child to be accepted as he is and to develop to the fullest whatever potential he brings into the world. However, it is of no help to disappointed parents (or their children) to say that they have no right to be disappointed. The first step in working innovatively with our children is to face up realistically to the situation and all our feelings about it. That done, we are in a position to look for positive factors and build well on them.

Every handicap presents its own special challenges to the child and to his family. It may necessitate special training of one kind or another. Sometimes it requires institutionalization. Depending on the severity of the handicap, the child may or may not be expected eventually to lead a relatively normal life. Coming to terms with what can and cannot be expected is frequently difficult for parents and may require expert counseling.

There may be a temptation to go from professional to professional with the hope of hearing a more favorable prognosis or turning up a new treatment—surgical, psychological, or medicinal. There are times when getting another opinion is justified, but this is not a course to pursue indefinitely, even if one has the money to do so. Generally one is much better off if, when a new professional is consulted, arrangements are made for the new person to have access to the records and opinions of all professionals who have been seen previously.

Accepting Our Children and Ourselves

There is a difference between accepting people the way they presently are and settling for this as being the outside limits of what they can ever become. A paramount aim of this book has been to try to help parents feel this distinction in their bones.

Tomorrow is always another day. People change, even after they are well into middle years. Circumstances also change. It is self-defeating to expect miracles of life or of any individual, but it is equally self-defeating to assume that the way things are now is the way ·they must always be.

Our needs and our children's needs mesh differently as we and they grow. In general, our children should become able to do and to give more with the passage of time. Yet there will be exceptions that we and they will have to ride with. They may sometimes be asked to give beyond their years, which can make them proud. We may sometimes need to find depths of patience that we did not think we had or feel we had to have, which can enlarge us.

Nobody can promise anybody a rose garden. Much that happens to all of us will depend upon the society in which we live. Yet if we and our children can manage to be accepting of each other, and of ourselves, ask enough but not too much of each other, and of ourselves, family life will be a more stimulating and growth-provoking experience for all concerned.

Bibliography and Suggested Reading

1 The Expert in Each of Us

Child Study Association of America, ed., with commentary by Anna W. M. Wolf. *A Reader for Parents: A Selection of Creative Literature About Childhood*. New York: W. W. Norton & Co., 1963.

This out-of-print book is worth looking for in the library.

Mayer, Greta, and Hoover, Mary. *When Children Need Special Help with Emotional Problems* (pamphlet). New York: Child Study Association of America, 1961.

Includes a description of the conventional kinds of special help available and how to go about getting a qualified practitioner.

Perlman, Helen. *Social Role and Personality*. Chicago: University of Chicago Press, 1968.

A gifted social worker discusses the multiple roles of men and women and how the healthy person can continue to grow in adult life.

Rogers, Carl R. *Carl Rogers on Encounter Groups*. New York: Harper & Row, 1970.

A sane description by a prominent therapist of what this approach to self-awareness has to offer.

2 The World We Live In

Bronfenbrenner, Urie. *Two Worlds of Childhood: U.S. and U.S.S.R.* New York: Russell Sage Foundation, 1970.

Ehrlich, Paul R., Ph.D., and Anne H. *Population, Re-*

sources, *Environment: Issues in Human Ecology.* San Francisco: W. H. Freeman, 1970.

Hoopes, Ned E., ed. *Who Am I? Essays on the Alienated* (paperback). Dell Publishing Co., Inc., 1969.

James, Howard. *Children in Trouble.* New York: David McKay Co., 1970.
Exposé of what goes on in facilities for youthful delinquents, orphans, and neglected and abused children.

Lady Allen of Hurtwood. *Planning for Play.* Cambridge: M.I.T. Press, 1968.
Splendidly illustrated roundup of information on planning playgrounds and play programs and providing opportunities for casual play.

Mead, Margaret. *Cultural Commitment: A Study of the Generation Gap.* New York: Doubleday & Co., Inc., Natural History Press, 1970.
Entertaining and provocative analysis of what the young need from their elders in this era of rapid social change.

Milner, Esther, et al. *Dialogue on Women* (paperback). New York: Bobbs-Merrill Co., Inc., 1967.
Compact, informative, and ahead of its time.

Silberman, Charles E. *Crisis in the Classroom.* New York: Random House, 1970.
Comprehensive discussion of problems and possible solutions.

Skolnick, Arlene S. and Jerome H. *Family in Transition.* New York: Little Brown & Co., 1971.
Wide-ranging source book; raises profound questions.

Thelen, Herbert A. *Dynamics of Groups at Work.* Chicago: University of Chicago Press, 1954.
Excellent introduction to what makes groups function constructively and possible roles of the leader.

Toffler, Alvin. *Future Shock.* New York: Random House, 1970.
Useful exposition of the effects of rapid social and technological change.

3 Preparing for a New Baby

Goodrich, Frederick W., Jr., M.D. *Preparing for Childbirth: A Manual for Expectant Parents*. Rev. ed. Englewood Cliffs, N.J.: Prentice-Hall, Inc., 1966.
Complete and sensible guide to "natural childbirth."

Hoffman, Martin L. and Lois W., eds. *Review of Child Development Research*. vol. 1. New York: Russell Sage Foundation, 1964.
Intended for professionals, but the section on the relative merits of breast- and bottlefeeding will reassure any mother.

LaLeche League International. *The Womanly Art of Breastfeeding*. Rev. ed., 1968.
Overly sentimental and evangelical, but packed with practical tips for women who have decided to breastfeed.

Maternity Center Association. *Guide for Expectant Parents* (paperback), 1969.
Question-and-answer format. Obtainable from the Association, 48 East 92nd Street, New York, N.Y. 10028.

————. *Preparation for Childbearing*. Rev. ed., 1972.
Handbook on preparing for "natural childbirth."

————. *A Baby Is Born: The Picture Story of a Baby from Conception Through Birth*. Rev. ed., 1964.

Spock, Benjamin, M.D. *Baby and Child Care* (paperback). Rev. ed. New York: Pocket Books, 1968.

Twins' Mothers Club of Bergen County, N.J. *And Then There Were Two: A Handbook for Mothers and Fathers of Twins* (pamphlet). Rev. ed. New York: Child Study Association of America, 1971.

4 No Parent Is Perfect

Geist, Harold. *A Child Goes to the Hospital: The Psychological Aspects of a Child Going to the Hospital*. Springfield, Ill.: Charles C. Thomas, 1965.

Hudson, Ian, M.D., and Thomas, Gordon. *What to Do Until the Doctor Comes*. Princeton: Vertex, 1970.

Kubler-Ross, Elisabeth, M.D. *On Death and Dying.* New York: The Macmillan Co., 1969.
Profound analysis of the "stages" through which a dying person passes in coming to terms with death.
Mayer, Greta, and Hoover, Mary. *When Children Need Special Help with Emotional Problems* (pamphlet). New York: Child Study Association of America, 1961.
Ruina, Edith. *Moving: A Common-Sense Guide to Relocating Your Family.* New York: Funk & Wagnalls, Inc., 1970.
Wolf, Anna W. M. *Helping Your Child to Understand Death* (pamphlet). Rev. ed. New York: Child Study Association of America, 1972.

5   What Makes Johnny "Behave"?

Bandura, Albert, and Walters, Richard H. *Adolescent Aggression: A Study of the Influence of Child-Training Practices and Family Interrelationships.* New York: Ronald Press Co., 1959.
Very detailed, technical report of a study comparing a group of delinquent boys with a group of nondelinquents having the same racial and class background.
Helfer, Ray E., M.D., and Kempe, E. Henry, M.D., eds. *The Battered Child.* Chicago: University of Chicago Press, 1968.

6   Parental Example: How It Rubs Off

Easton, David, and Dennis, Jack. *Children in the Political System: Origins of Political Legitimacy.* New York: McGraw-Hill, Inc., 1969.
Detailed study of the political attitudes of 12,000 American schoolchildren of ages 7 to 14.
Lee, Roy S. *Your Growing Child and Religion: A Psychological Account* (paperback). New York: The Mac-

millan Co., 1963. An English chaplain and psychologist suggests that parents' handling of their young children is the crucial element in their religious education.

8 Tapping a Child's Potential
Bland, Jane Cooper. *Art of the Young Child: Understanding and Encouraging Creative Growth in Children Three to Five.* New York: Museum of Modern Art, distr. by New York Graphic Society, 1968.
Hart, Harold H., ed. *Summerhill: For and Against.* New York: Hart Publishing Co., 1970.
Fifteen essays by educators, psychologists, and sociologists, on the "Summerhill" approach to education.
Kubie, Lawrence, M.D. *Neurotic Distortions of the Creative Process.* Lawrence: University of Kansas Press, 1958.
A psychoanalytical interpretation, not easy reading but lucid, of the roots of what we call creativity.
Sheehy, Emma A. *Children Discover Music and Dance* (paperback). New York: Teachers College, 1968.
Smith, Charles P., ed. *Achievement-Related Motives in Children.* New York: Russell Sage Foundation, 1969.
Research reports by eight psychologists and educators.
Thomas, Alexander, et al. *Temperament and Behavior Disorders in Children.* New York: New York University, 1968.
Report of a longitudinal study (10 years, 141 children) suggesting the range of children's temperamental differences and how an individual child's "fit" with his environment may affect his chances of realizing his potential.

9 The Beautiful Times
Provence, Sally, M.D., and Lipton, Rose, M.D. *Children in Institutions.* New York: International Universities Press, 1962.

Though written for a professional audience, a very clear, readable exposition of the way in which institutionalized babies may lose all capacity for joy and how this is interrelated with the capacity to respond in other ways.

10   Having the Children You Want—and No More

American Friends Service Committee: *Who Shall Live? Man's Control over Birth and Death* (paperback). New York: Hill & Wang, Inc., 1970.
Superb report on some of the most crucial and sensitive issues of the day, written with unusual clarity and compassion.

Glass, Robert H., M.D., and Kase, Nathan G., M.D. *Woman's Choice: A Guide to Contraception, Fertility, Abortion, and Menopause.* New York: Basic Books, Inc., 1970.

Grover, John W., M.D. *V.D.: the ABC's.* Englewood Cliffs, N.J.: Prentice-Hall, Inc., 1971.
Comprehensive and singularly free of moralizing and scare tactics.

Kadushin, Alfred. *Adopting Older Children.* New York: Columbia University Press, 1970. A research report, but not unreadable and possibly of interest to couples considering this step.

Lader, Lawrence. *A Guide to Abortion Laws in the United States* (pamphlet). New York: Planned Parenthood–World Population, periodically updated. This reprint of an article in *Redbook,* June, 1971, gives a state-by-state rundown of facilities and sources of information for legal abortion. Available for 25¢ a copy from the organization at 810 Seventh Avenue, New York, N.Y. 10019.

Le Shan, Eda J. *You and Your Adopted Child.* New York: Public Affairs Pamphlets, 1958.
Still fine on attitudes of adopted children and their parents.

11 Our Needs in Perspective

Albrecht, Margaret. A *Complete Guide for the Working Mother* (paperback). New York: Award Books, 1967.

Brecher, Ruth and Edward, eds. *An Analysis of Human Sexual Response*. New York: Little Brown & Co., 1966. A skillful interpretation of the classic Masters-Johnson research on sex.

Buckler, Beatrice. *Living with a Mentally Retarded Child: A Primer for Parents*. New York: Hawthorn Books, Inc., 1971.
Very simple, practical information plus an unusually full and valuable listing of facilities and resources.

Despert, J. Louise, M.D. *Children of Divorce*. Rev. ed. New York: Doubleday & Co., Inc., 1953. Dated but still may be more valuable than anything else you can find on helping children weather divorce in healthy fashion.

Kirk, Samuel A., et al. *You and Your Retarded Child: A Manual for Parents of Retarded Children*. Rev. ed. Palo Alto: Pacific Books, 1968.
Good on care of child at home and deciding whether residential treatment is needed.

May, Elizabeth Eckhardt, et al. *Homemaking for the Handicapped*. New York: Dodd, Mead & Co., 1966.
Authoritative, helpfully illustrated guide to assist the disabled adult in caring for children and a home.

Robinson, Frank Bennett. *Introduction to Stuttering*. Englewood Cliffs, N.J.: Prentice-Hall, Inc., 1964.

Rubin, Isadore, Ph.D. *Sexual Life After Sixty*. New York: Basic Books, Inc., 1965.

Sherwin, Robert Veit. *Compatible Divorce*. New York: Crown Publishers, Inc., 1969.
Combines psychological insight with legal expertise in suggesting how divorce can be handled to avoid the financial and psychological destruction of a family.

248

Smith, Bert Kruger. *Your Nonlearning Child: His World of Upside-Down*. Boston: Beacon Press, 1968.

In addition to cluing parents in to the way the world is for children with perceptual and other disabilities, this book offers suggestions for getting appropriate help.

Spock, Benjamin, M.D., and Lerrigo, Marion O. *Caring for Your Disabled Child*. New York: The Macmillan Co., 1965.

Thompson, Helen. *The Successful Step-parent*. New York: Harper & Row, 1966.

Wallis, J. H. *Sexual Harmony in Marriage*. New York: Roy Publishers, Inc., 1966.

Witty and wise discussion of what the author, a British marriage counselor, calls "the sexual conversation" between men and women from adolescence on.

Wright, Beatrice A. *Physical Disability: A Psychological Approach*. New York: Harper & Row, 1960.

A pioneering book, focusing on the ways in which emotional health can be nurtured to make for maximum realization of potential.

Suggested Additional Reading

Albrecht, Margaret. *Parents and Teen-agers: Getting Through to Each Other*. New York: Parents' Magazine Press, 1972.

Gilbert, Sara D. *Three Years to Grow*. New York: Parents' Magazine Press, 1972.

Minton, Lynn. *Growing into Adolescence*. New York: Parents' Magazine Press, 1972.

Mogal, Doris P. *Character in the Making*. New York: Parents' Magazine Press, 1972.

Neisser, Edith G. *Primer for Parents of Preschoolers*. New York: Parents' Magazine Press, 1972.

Index

abortion, 55, 57–58, 208–209
acceptance, child's need for, 46
Adams, Dr. Paul, 56
Adopting Older Children, 213
adoption, 188, 212–214, 237
advice, conflicting, 26, 77
affection, lack of, 175
aggression, 88–89
Albrecht, Margaret, 46
American Board of Pediatrics, 64
anger, 181–182
apathy, 53
approval, child's need for, 46
attention, child's need for, 82
attitudes
  changing, 17
  child's, 107–108, 130
authority
  attitudes toward, 107–108
  exercising, 17
  tolerance for, 140

baby, preparing for, 54–77
baby-sitting, cooperative, 218
basal body temperature, 204–206, 210
Battered Child, The, 111
behavior
  accepting consequences of, 111, 171, 176
  adult, confusing to child, 128–129
  child, 97–118
  clinging to babyish, 155, 157
  conscious, controlled by ego, 83
  controlling, 182
  defiant, 17
  misconstruing, 22
  parental, 125–126, 133–134
  problem, 80, 81, 84–88, 176
  reading a child's 145–147
  as test of handling child, 25
  unconscious, id and superego in, 83
birth control, 43, 188–214
birth defects, 189–190
blind spots, 19, 31
bossiness, 17, 86, 88–89
bottle-feeding, 61
Bowlby, Dr. John, 175
breast-feeding, 61–62, 70

camp, 22, 160–161
Camus, Albert, 38
challenges
  artificial, 160
  child must face, 226
  child's response to, 156–157
  of child's handicap, 239
  evaluating, 162–163
  as help to child, 159
  of times, 33, 41–53
change, social, 41–42, 43, 53
checkup, medical, 63, 195
child
  handicapped, 238
  the "happy," 175–176
  impact of divorce on, 236
  institutionalized, 175
  only, 192
  vulnerability of, 108–109
childbirth, 71–74

beginning of labor (illus.), 73

end of first stage (illus.), 73

natural, 71–72, 75

risks of, 189–190

second stage of labor, 74, (illus.), 74

child care, cooperative, 45

child guidance clinic, 29–30

children
ideal number of, 192
spacing of, 189–190

Children's Rights, 56

Clergy Consultation Service on Adoption, 208

clinic
child guidance, 30
mental health, 29, 81
prenatal, 58–60, 65
well-baby, 63

Clomid, 211

clues, sensitivity to, 23, 25

communication, 135–149, 238
with child, 25
honest, 42–43
"instant," 48
of prospective parents, 68

community
activity, 35, 36, 39
"belonging" in, 47
child in the, 53
spirit, need for, 44–46

competence, child's level of, 154–155

confrontation, 118, 141

conscience, 83, 106, 107
See also Inner controls

contraceptive, 213
diaphragm (illus.), 199
foams (illus.), 201

types of, 193–208

cooperation, 14, 17, 39, 43

counselor, 29, 58, 239

creativity, 166–170, 174

cues, child's, 16, 25

danger, child's awareness of, 99

death, in family, 79, 82

decision-making
by child, 80
parental, 95–96

"demand" feeding, 70, 101

Demerol, in natural childbirth, 72

depression, 38, 176

determination, as ego strength, 84

development
intellectual, 191
stages of, 152–154
stimulation toward, 161–162
uneven, 155–156, 157–158

differences, individual, 20, 48

disabilities, congenital, 164–166
See also Handicaps

discipline, 97, 105
approach to, 100
firmness in, 114
and mothers, 116–117
in one-parent family, 117
See also Punishment

distraction, as technique, 18

divorce, 27, 158, 235–236

doctor, choice of, 71

drive, instinctual, 83

drugs, 23, 42–43
fertility, 211

ecology, 33, 35, 39, 189

education, 39, 80

lock-step system of, 168
volunteer work in, 35
woman's role in, 43
egalitarianism, in sex, 132
ego, 83
"emotional flatness," 182
emotional health, 31, 37, 79,
    82–83, 175, 180, 236–
    237
emotions, 182–187
empathy, 14, 15, 16, 17, 23,
    24, 25, 26, 52, 138, 222,
    228
employment opportunities, 43,
    80
encounter groups, 30–31
environment, 20, 28
    capacity to cope with, 49
    healthy, 34–35, 53
estrogen, 193, 202
example, parental, 119–134
    teaching through, 185–187
experience of childhood, using,
    17–18
expertise, parental, 13–31

Fallopian tubes, tying of, 206
family
    extended, 45, 236
    large, 192
    limiting size of, 188
    nuclear, 45, 123
    one-parent, 236–238
"family doctor," 63
family planning, 188–214
father, sharing child care, 229–
    230
fertility drugs, 211
flexibility, 15–16, 25–26, 43
    as ego strength, 84

learned from role model, 122
freedom to make choices, 102–
    104
friends, child's choice of, 46
frustration, 51, 52
    protection against, 101
fun, linked to responsibility,
    187

Gilbert, Sara D., 70
Glass, Robert H., M.D., 204
growth
    cognitive, 191
    marital and personal, in preg-
        nancy, 56
    master pattern in, 152–154
    psychological, 28
    variations in, 157–158
guidance, acceptance of, 17

guilt, parental, 58, 79, 80, 81
gynecology, 60

handicaps, 239–240
hardships, unavoidable, 78–79
health
    care of, 80
    emotional, 31, 37, 79, 82–
        83, 93, 175, 180, 236–237
    mental, 79, 82, 174
Helfer, Ray E., M.D., 111
help, professional, 28–29, 30,
    86, 176, 239–240
holidays
    impact on child, 178–180
    significance of, 172–174
hormonal balance, 193, 196
hormonal therapy, in infertil-
    ity, 211
hospital, choosing, 58–59

humor
   in communication, 141
   in coping with stress, 51
   as tonic in pregnancy, 57
husband
   and emotional strain, in pregnancy, 67–68
   and wife as team, 66

id, 83
identification
   with child, 17
   with parents, 130
identity, child's sense of, 37, 38, 46, 47
   sexual, 129–132
inconsistencies, explaining, 126
independence, 98, 100, 102–105
infertility, 188, 209–212
influence, parental, 32, 43
inner controls, 108
   as child-rearing goal, 98, 105–107
   undermining child's, 184
   See also Conscience
interests
   conflicting, 35
      of id and superego, 83
   sharing of, 15
intrauterine device (IUD), 196–197
involvement, importance of, 37, 38–39

jealousy, 109
joyousness, 181–182, 187
   capacity to feel, 173–175, 176–177
   as ego strength, 84
juvenile delinquents, 111

Kadushin, Alfred, 213
Kase, Nathan G., M.D., 204
Kempe, C. Henry, M.D., 111
Kubie, Dr. Lawrence, 168

learning
   motivation for, 39
   problems of, 29
limitations
   imaginary, 163
   parental, 79
limits, 100–110
   child's understanding of, 105
   designed for safety, 187
   giving in on, 114–116
   parental, 222
listener, good, 140–141
listen, when child does not, 141–143
listlessness, in babies, 174

male sterilization (illus.), 207
marathons, 30–31
marriage, fulfillment in, 231–235
mental health, 29, 81, 82–84
   factors in, 174
minority group, 32, 35
mistakes
   of parents, 78–96
   paying price for, 112
money, 18–19
moodiness, in adolescence, 176
mortality rate, 49, 189–190, 194–195
"mothering," essential to growth, 191
mother, new, 64–65, 75–76
mother, working, 95, 229–231
music, 22, 167

natural childbirth, 59, 71–72, 75
needs of parents, 215–240
neighbors, 45, 46
Neisser, Edith G., 70
newborn, described, 75
"no," child's, 16
nursery school, 159–160
nutrition, 47

obstetrician, 58–59, 60, 71, 190
one-parent family, 117, 236–238
only child, 192
overpermissiveness, 110
overprotection, 99, 224–226

parents
  authoritarian, 109
  child's faith in, 225–226
  competing for child's affection, 235
  disappointments of, 238–240
  emotional maturity of, 233
  emotions of, 186
  example of, 119–134
  expertise of, 13–31
  fulfillment of, 227–234
  identifying with child, 227
  limitations of, 20, 90–92
  mistakes of, 78–96
  needs of, 215–240
  as role models, 119–124

pediatrician, 63–64
peers, child's, 46–47, 102
Perls, Fritz, 28
permissiveness, 98, 108–110
perspective

  on dangers, 49
  on parental needs, 215–240
  on past, 27
pets, 24–25
Planned Parenthood—World Population, 208
politics
  women in, 43
  young people in, 35–36
pollution, 33, 36–37, 43, 49
population
  explosion, 43, 50, 213
  growth of, 33, 189
potential, child's, 150–171
poverty, 19, 43, 192–193
pregnancy
  diet in, 77
  effect of, on emotions, 67
  feelings about, 55–58
  German measles in, 60–61
  goals in, 76–77
  medication in, 60
  mortality rate in, 194
  reading during, 70
  recovery from, 190
  Thalidomide in, 60–61
  timing of, 189
  unwanted, 192–193, 208, 212
prenatal care, 58–60
pressure
  competitiveness as, 171
  unavoidable, 159
  See also Stress
priorities
  in pregnancy, 77
  reordering personal, 52–53, 116
progesterone, 210
progestin, 193, 202–203

projection, 22–24
psychology, of groups, 36
puberty, age of, 47
punishment, 88–89, 98, 110–113, 117
    artificial challenge as, 160
    physical, 19, 78, 91, 106
pushing of child, 160–162, 168, 228, 171

rage, 23, 38, 109
reading, 14–15
regression, 86, 156
relationship
    man-woman, 43
    of parents and pediatrician, 64
    with parents in pregnancy, 56–57
resentment
    parental, 186, 222–226
    right to feel, 184
respect
    for child, 137–138
    mutual, 14, 177
responsibility, 122, 176, 187
rights of others, respect for, 98, 101–102, 122, 143, 176, 187, 215–216
role models, 171
    effectiveness of, 123
    other than parents, 185
    parents as, 119–124, 177–178
    sexual, 129–132
    teachers as, 120–121, 122
"rooming-in," 59, 70–71

safety, 97–100
schools, 33, 34, 39, 43
self-awareness, 30–31

self-confidence
    as ego strength, 84
    parental, 26
self-control, parental, 185–186
self-esteem, 98, 99–102
    nurturing, 151–152
self-image, 162, 170
self-interest, parental, 215–216
self-reliance, parental, 49
self-understanding, 28, 30–31
sensitivity training, 30–31
sexual identity, 129–132
sharing, 24, 101, 177
    in baby care, 66–67
    of interests, 15
    of worries, 224–226
sibling rivalry, 86–89
society
    active role in, 34–35
    attitudes of, toward women, 43, 44
    and authority, 107
    child's view of, 170
    efforts to change, 38, 53
    as factor in child-rearing, 80, 171
    goal of, 239
    mobile, 44–45, 46
    parents blamed by, 80
    role in tapping child's potential, 169–170
    sports-oriented, 162
sorrow, 23, 181–182
"spoiling," 78
sterilization, 196, 206–208, (illus.), 207
stimulation
    essential to growth, 191
    intellectual, 94
storytelling, 94–95

Stranger, The, 38
stress
  avoidable, 52, 158
  child's ability to withstand, 81, 82
  living with, 50–51
  parental, 225–226
success, 170–171
superego, 83
  See also Conscience

talents, 166–170
teacher
  anger with, 183
  interested, 82
  as role model, 120–121, 122
  unsympathetic, 79
technology, 34, 35, 41–42, 49, 50
television, 41, 47
tensions, parental, 226
  See also Stress
Thalidomide, 60–61
therapist, 29, 30, 185
thermal shift (illus.), 205
toilet training, 155, 158
touch groups, 30–31

trauma, childhood, 81
truth, 124–125, 224–226
tubal ligation (illus.), 207

values
  American, 170–171
  confusion about, 143
  rethinking, 52
vas deferens, tying of, 206
vasectomy, 206, (illus.) 207
Visiting Nurse Service, 65
volunteer work, 35, 36

weaknesses, accepting, 163–165
white lies, 124–125, 126, 127
Wittgenstein, Ludwig, 167
Woman's Choice, 204
women
  changing role of, 43
women's liberation movement, 44, 231–232
worries, sharing with children, 224–226